Alfred C Bossom's American Architecture 1903–1926

ALFRED C BOSSOM'S AMERICAN ARCHITECTURE 1903–1926

Dennis Sharp

with contributions from Peter Wylde and Martha Caldwell

Book Art, London
1984

Frontispiece

Alfred C. Bossom (1881–1965) with his studio model of the cresting design for the Liberty Bank Building, Buffalo. Photograph probably taken in 1924.

Catalogue edited and designed by Dennis Sharp
Research: Peter Wylde
Secretarial Assistance: Nancy Jackson
Photography: Jeremy Finlay
Exhibition designed by Dennis Sharp Architects, London

Bossom Exhibition

The exhibition 'Building to the Skies: Alfred C Bossom's American Architecture 1903–26' opened at the Building Centre Gallery, Store Street, London on April 3, 1984. The exhibition designed and co-ordinated by Dennis Sharp Architects, London and Hertford. The exhibitions will be shown at various centres in the USA in 1985 including Washington DC, New York, and Texas, with support from the British Council.

ISBN No 0 947648 00 3

Published by Book Art, 4 All Saints Street, London N1 9RL
Printed in Great Britain by White Crescent Press Ltd, Luton

Cover Picture

Details of panel designed by
Alfred C Bossom for a lacquered cabinet, 1928

CONTENTS

Foreword

Sir Hugh Casson, KCVO, RDI, FRIBA
President, Royal Academy

The past, we know, was once the future, with its usual promised cargo of hope and despair. To those of us qualifying in the early Thirties, there seemed to be plenty of both in the world of architecture. The great post-war housing boom was coming to a standstill. There was a world economic slump. British industry was subsiding into a collapse as dramatic as the disintegration of the Empire. In this dispiriting confusion architecture seemed to us to pause irresolute. The grand old men – Lutyens, Baker, Blomfield among them – continued to vamp their variations on a classical theme. 'Pswedish' seemed to be the preferred style of the establishment – copper-roofed town halls, sash-windowed hospitals, vita-glazed schools, but here and there the first tiny white lambs of the modern movement – 'Hooray' we cried – were being coaxed shakily to their feet under the solemn and magisterial guidance of such distinguished refugees as Gropius, Mendelsohn, Breuer, Lubetkin.

Work was thin on the ground, optimists rarely encountered. Unshakeably one of them, however, was the architect Alfred Bossom, whose life and work is the subject of this exhibition.

Bossom had recently returned from America to live in England and when, in about 1935, I met him – at some occasion at the Royal Society of Arts – he seemed physically to embody within his tiny frame all the dynamism of the New World. It was my first peek into the corridors of power and I was ill-at-ease. I knew he was rich, that he lived in a castle and gave white-tie'd parties in his London mansion. His, I knew, was not my world. But I was instantly disarmed. He was genial, interested, bright-eyed, almost incandescent with energy, and ravenously curious about everything. These are qualities to which it is impossible not to respond, and they drove him at top speed through his life. At the time I knew little of his background. I believed (wrongly) that he was American. I had been told (wrongly) that he had invented the skyscraper. I learned however quickly from what he said that he had dedicated his professional life to exploiting to the full every advance in building techniques and site organisation, and advised me to do the same. Not surprisingly, this ability, I discovered later, had brought him great success in the boom years at the beginning of this century. He specialised in the design of Banks, welcoming the opportunity to express the required impression of permanence and reliability by speaking in a conservative language and with the best materials that could be afforded, but always looking for ways of doing it more quickly and more efficiently. As a designer he was equally pertinacious. In his search for a true 'American' style he looked beyond Rome to the civilisations of Central America and in particular, as this exhibition so clearly shows, to Guatemala. Here he found and developed a personal design style which – given an extra spurt by the Paris Exhibition of 1925 – contained, it could be claimed, the seeds of Art Deco recently rediscovered with such enthusiasm by architects and historians on both sides of the Atlantic.

On two points therefore, Alfred Bossom emerges as something of a pioneer, first in his notable contribution to the skyscraper-style of the early 20th century, now so widely studied and admired, and secondly in his relentless pursuit of efficient building techniques. Sadly, after his return to England he never practised as an architect, preferring to devote his energies to public service. His success in this field was such that he is today more generally remembered by his political achievements than by his architecture. I hope this exhibition will help to correct this balance.

January 1984

Preface

'The great innovation wrought by this new type of building (the skyscraper) was that it did away with walls . . . as supports and additions to structural strength.'

'It is doubly natural that America and no other country should have been the birthplace of the skyscraper.'

'It is almost a law of architectural necessity that the Americans in stretching their buildings skywards should come to use the same treatments of flat surfaces, set-backs and ornamented silhouettes . . . as the Mayans in Mexico.'

Such words as these clearly express some of the enterprising, and often original ideas, of Alfred C Bossom (1881–1965) whose work is examined in detail in this publication and the accompanying exhibition 'Building to the Skies'.

Bossom has over the past few years become increasingly valued in the US as an important, if somewhat neglected, pioneer of the American skyscraper architecture of the first quarter of this century. This aspect of his career remains virtually unknown in Britain where – understandably perhaps – he has always been more closely associated with politics and public life. Whilst he never gave up his interest and commitment to architecture and the arts he was more in demand in Britain as a chairman and patron than as a practising architect. In fact he never practised again after he returned to Britain in 1926 ostensibly to take advantage of educational opportunities for his sons.

Born in the Caledonian Road, Islington Bossom's early professional life in America is a great success story. In a series of articles in this publication an attempt has been made to trace his early period in the US and to show through many previously unpublished drawings and photographs the breadth of Bossom's American experience.

This re-evaluation is long overdue. Its importance to the knowledge and understanding of the history of American skyscraper design is constantly being underlined by demands for information from state, county and city conservation officers who, sensing that they may have an important structure ready for landmarking find they have little or no knowledge of the architect 'Alfred C Bossom of Fifth Avenue, New York'. Some of these officials have been able to update much of the information on the present condition of Bossom's buildings for this book and exhibition.

The lack of interest in Alfred Bossom's architecture in Britain has been, I would suggest, largely due to his prominence as a Conservative politician over many years. If he has been remembered for his contribution to architecture it has been on three main counts: the steering through Parliament of the Architects' Registration Bill, his involvement in the Portal Mission on house prefabrication in the US, 1943–44, and the publication of a book which hitherto has been treated as something of an oddity amongst the architectural writings of the 1930s. The book, *Building to the Skies: The Romance of the Skyscraper*, was published in London and New York in 1934; it was a decade too late. In America the building boom was over by the mid-30s, killed stone dead by the slump. In Britain no one wanted to build skyscrapers, except perhaps those committed to the idealism implicit in Le Corbusier's Utopian visions. The book was totally out of phase with contemporary attitudes in Britain. The Corbusian and Bauhaus revolution were well underway and the manifestations of puritanical form-giving precluded anyone seeing Bossom's message or creative originality – at all clearly. The mirror constantly being held up to the past by the so-called Georgian revivalists was equally darkened. As to those advocating the establishment of conducive communities along the lines of Letchworth and Welywn Garden Cities any ideas that pursued the construction of tall buildings of any kind (however romantic) were anathema. Of all the vested interest groups fighting off low scale ribbon development the garden city wallahs – whose own idols had achieved most success in Colonial cities – would no doubt have seen Bossom's skyscraper book as a distinct threat to their own romantic city notions. Bossom himself believed, in fact, that the *light* was not right for skyscrapers in Britain.

It is hoped that this exhibition will now place Alfred Bossom's work in an international context and enhance his Anglo-American reputation. It has been largely made possible by the response of his own family to a probative article originally published in the *AA Quarterly* produced with the help of a former AA student Peter Wylde. His research work has again proved invaluable on this project. Alfred Bossom's son, the Hon Sir Clive Bossom Bt, has most generously allowed his own family's enthusiasm for a reassessment of his father's American career to show itself by sponsoring this new research as well as this publication. His encouragement and obvious joy in discovering new facts on his father has made the job most worthwhile.

Thanks are also due to the Director of the London Building Centre, Mr John George, for supporting the Bossom exhibition when it was little more than a germ of an idea. Diana Collett of the Centre has also been helpful and eased many of our problems of display.

I would also like to acknowledge the work and help provided by Jeremy Finlay for his outstanding photographic work carried out with an efficiency that would have pleased Bossom himself, Wendy Aldhous for her bibliographical work and advice, the unstinting help provided by Mrs Nancy Jackson in typing out drafts and manuscripts often against the clock as well as to our American colleague Prof Martha Caldwell of James Madison University, Virginia who has applied her great skills to the tasks of delineation, documentation and scholarship initially in pursuit of her own interest in Alfred Bossom and now for this publication.

Finally, Sir Clive Bossom wishes to express his special thanks to his wife Barbara and his sons Bruce, Andrew and James who have 'beavered away' and helped to retrace over sixty years of Alfred Bossom's architectural life. With me, Sir Clive reiterates his warmest appreciation to Peter Wylde for his painstaking research, thus making it possible to present such a wide selection of his father's work.

Dennis Sharp
Epping Green, Hertford, UK
February 1984

Memoir of Alfred C Bossom

The Hon Sir Clive Bossom, Bt

In his long life, my father enjoyed two entirely different careers. The first as an architect in America, the second as a politician in England.

In 1906, aged twenty-two and having done brilliantly at the Royal Academy of Arts, he went to America as a young British architect to design a housing scheme for the Carnegie Steel Mills in Pittsburgh, Pennsylvania. Years later he told me that he had only intended to stay a few months, but it soon became clear to him that America was the land of opportunity. It was here that his career began to take off.

In 1910 he fell in love and married a young American girl, Emily Bayne. My mother soon became deeply involved in her husband's work. As the son-in-law of Samuel Bayne, President of The Seaboard National Bank of New York, my father was well placed to be invited to design new buildings for the Bank.

During this time, the Pell family asked him to help restore the historic landmark of Fort Ticonderoga on Lake Champlain in northern New York State, built by the French in 1755. My parents spent a working holiday at the Fort, camping in the only room that was habitable. One night the bride, while reading in bed, was startled to see a bearded old man breathing heavily on the frosted window. My father was sent off in haste to deal with the intruder who turned out to be an inquisitive billy goat. Attracted by the light in the deserted building it had walked across the ice of the frozen Lake Champlain.

Throughout his life, my father had a passion for collecting unusual artifacts. He was fascinated by the West Coast Indians of British Columbia, whom he regarded as the most interesting group of aborigines within the British Commonwealth. Whilst returning from a trip to the Klondyke goldfields, he was tremendously attracted to the work of the Kwakiutls, the Haidas and the Tsimshians and began to collect their work. For the next forty years he continued to accumulate totem poles, wooden canoes, masks, grease bowls, shale dishes, cooking utensils, tools – in fact specimens of everything they made or used in their daily lives.

Many years later he brought back to England this collection of some five thousand pieces, where it was on loan to the Imperial Institute and to the British Museum. Today, 'The Bossom Collection' is on permanent show in the new National Museum of Man in Ottawa where I was very proud to see part of it on display when I visited Canada with a Parliamentary Delegation in 1971.

My parents were both very artistic and, on many occasions, combined their talents. A good example is their book *An Architectural Pilgrimage in Old Mexico* of 1924, in which my mother took the photographs while my father contributed the sketches. Having often travelled with him around Europe and parts of the Middle East, I know that he was always armed with a small sketch book and three or four coloured pencils. He would impulsively make me stop so that he could sketch anything from an entire building to a small ornate

doorway – or piece of ironwork – which caught his eye. At public Dinners during long speeches he would invariably make amusing – but never cruel – caricatures of the speaker and fellow guests on the back of the menus. I was always terrified he might leave them behind on the table!

My mother was musical and, for several years, was Treasurer of the New York Philharmonic. I will always remember being taken to concerts and operas as a small boy and being allowed to sit at the back of the box – hearing all but seeing nothing! Great artists such as Toscanini, Fürtwangler, Mengelberg would come to our home after their performances, and I had the excitement of meeting my musical heroes.

I will also never forget that amazing home of ours at 270 Park Avenue, New York. On stepping out of the elevator you had the magical illusion of entering a 17th century Spanish mansion, complete with whitewashed, domed ceilings, terracotta tiled floors, period furniture and richly ornate tapestries. On special occasions, such as musical receptions, the rooms would be lit by wrought iron candlesticks holding huge church candles. You would never have believed you were in the centre of New York. My father loved creating these illusions, and years later, when he was back in London, he slept in a Spanish bedroom and worked in an evocative Spanish style 'den'.

Design of a picture gallery for a country town. An early student project by Bossom c1899.

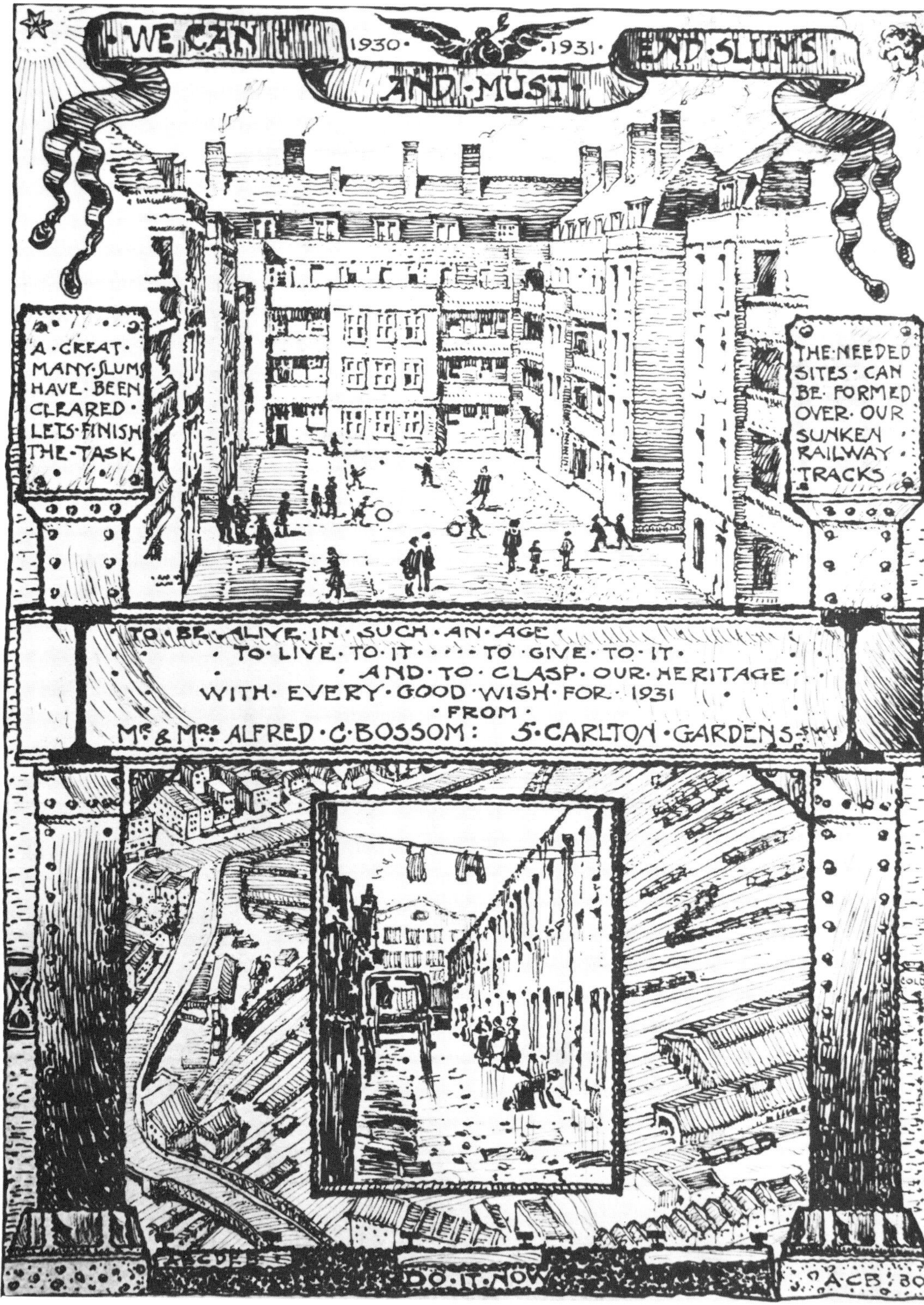
WE CAN
1930
1931
END SLUMS
AND MUST
A GREAT MANY SLUMS HAVE BEEN CLEARED LETS FINISH THE TASK
THE NEEDED SITES CAN BE FORMED OVER OUR SUNKEN RAILWAY TRACKS
TO BE ALIVE IN SUCH AN AGE
TO LIVE TO IT TO GIVE TO IT
AND TO CLASP OUR HERITAGE
WITH EVERY GOOD WISH FOR 1931
FROM
MR & MRS ALFRED C BOSSOM: 5 CARLTON GARDENS SW1
DO IT NOW
ACB 30

Two sketches from the Egyptian Sketch Book.

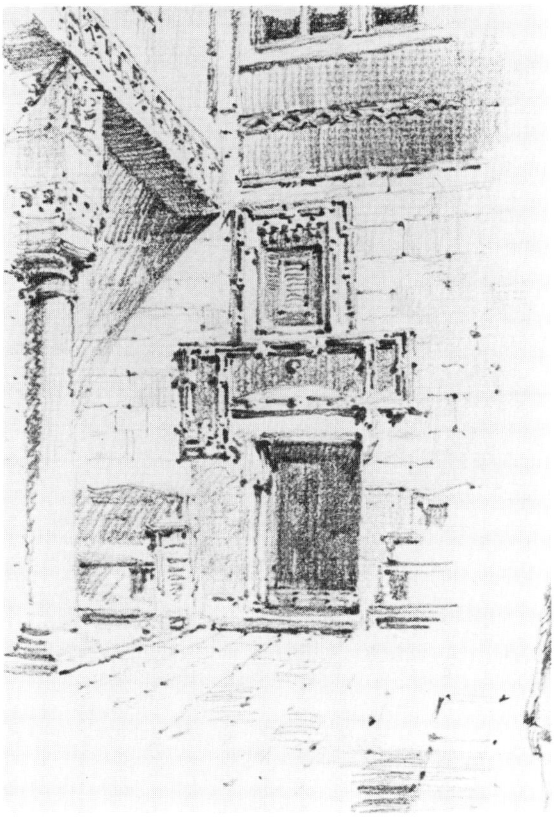

Although he was intensely proud and deeply grateful to have worked in America during this revolutionary period in architecture he remained British to the core. He was determined that his three sons should be brought up and educated in England. So in 1926, at the height of a most rewarding and successful career, he 'closed up shop' and brought his young family home to England. I am sure he would be delighted to know that two of his grandsons have followed his example by starting their working careers in the United States: Bruce in Houston and Andrew in New York. Looking back, I am sorry that he did not remain in America longer, as back in England he never again practised as an architect, and thereby, I feel, stifled some of his creative powers.

My father having settled his sons, Bruce, Doric, and myself, at various schools, then had to make up his mind what he was going to do. He was still a powerhouse of ideas and originality, but he could not see a way to practise architecture in Britain with his very different expertise. Of one thing he was convinced – skyscrapers were unsuitable for the British Isles. The temperament of the British did not appear to like high-rise buildings but preferred, as they still do, to live close to the ground. Skyscrapers, he said, needed a very clear, bright light and the British skies were never quite strong enough. Moreover, one very tall building by itself on a British skyline would stand out like a sore thumb. He believed that if the time ever came when high buildings would be built in Britain, then they should be sited together in groups.

So he turned his untapped energies to politics. He became a Conservative Parliamentary Candidate and unsuccessfully contested Central Hackney in 1927. He and my mother greatly enjoyed being 'blooded' in this difficult, but interesting seat. The same year he was co-opted onto the Housing Committee of the London County Council. In 1929 he became a London County Council Alderman and spearheaded the fight for slum clearance.

He successfully fought Maidstone in 1931 and entered the House of Commons, where he was to remain for the next 28 years. Tragically, in the following year, my mother and my elder brother were killed in a flying accident.

Having followed my father into politics, I know that he was greatly admired for the resolute way he represented his constituents. For most of his time in the House of Commons he was the only experienced architect there, contributing to his Profession by steering through Parliament The Architects Registration Bill of 1932.

In 1943 the Prime Minister, Sir Winston Churchill, sent him on a mission to America to look into prefabricated houses to replace those that

had been bombed in England. At the Fontana Dam in the vast Tennessee Valley he found temporary houses that were brought to the site in two halves. He brought back to England five different models and one hundred and seventy thousand 'prefabs', some of which are still standing, were erected all over the country to house the homeless.

My father took a very active interest in the Inter-Parliamentary Union, travelling extensively to many parts of the world. Before the 1939 War he visited the Baltic States several times, having a particular affection for Latvia, and in 1933 he became Founder and President of the Anglo-Baltic Society. Other countries with whom he had particularly close working relations were Belgium and Iran, becoming Chairman of both their Societies in 1956. Almost twenty years later I had the honour to follow the same path. Also, after the War, he launched the Anglo-Texan society which flourished for many years.

He was inexhaustible, and his capacity for work kept three secretaries working flat out. He founded the Modular Society, a new approach to standardisation in architecture, and worked hard with the Royal Society of Arts, first as Treasurer then as Chairman. Another of his great interests was with the Order of St John of Jerusalem, and he gave much time and energy to the re-building of their Eye Hospital in Jordan.

He was also very gregarious and, all his life, enjoyed bringing different groups of people together, insisting, quite rightly, that this made for better parties. His 'Eve of Parliament' parties at 5, Carlton Gardens, one of the last of the large London homes, will long be remembered. Years ago his predecessor as Member of Parliament for Maidstone, Lord Londonderry, used to give a very grand party before the Opening of each new Session of Parliament. My father tried to keep up this old Londonderry tradition. He built a great marquee with wooden floor and walls which he hung with tapestries, armour and other possessions brought from Allington Castle, our country home near Maidstone. At the evening reception, after their Dinner at 10 Downing Street, the Prime Minister and his Cabinet would arrive in white ties. The Members of Parliament and other guests wore black ties. At least this helped us to recognise who was who – except that the waiters also wore white ties! These receptions became very popular, particularly with Members' wives because it gave them a chance to meet their husbands' colleagues, which otherwise seldom happened. Although I have tried to follow my father in many of his interests developed during his long Parliamentary career, entertaining nine hundred thirsty people annually was an historic event which sadly had to die with him!

While he was South Eastern Area Chairman of the Conservative Party my father tried to help and guide young Parliamentary Candidates. As I was Chairman of the Conservative Parliamentary Candidates for five years, this was a great help as he allowed me to use 5, Carlton Gardens for our gatherings. During his Chairmanship a certain Margaret Roberts was one young Conservative who caught his attention and whom he encouraged. In fact she held her wedding reception at our home. Ten years later I was fortunate to be Mrs Margaret Thatcher's first Parliamentary Private Secretary when she became a Junior Minister in 1960. How happy my father would be today, having predicted that she would go far in politics!

My father continued to indulge his passion for collecting. In England it was an interesting collection of armour, snuff boxes in the form of tiny wooden shoes, powder horns and painted policemen's truncheons. In North Africa and Jordan he collected old jewellery which once had adorned the Bedouins. Yet alongside his interest in these antiquities he had also a very forward outlook in contemporary art. I remember when one day, after a very good lunch, my mother and father visited the old Leicester Square Gallery in London. They walked down opposite sides of the room and ended up together in front of the highly controversial statue of 'Genesis' by Jacob Epstein. The both said

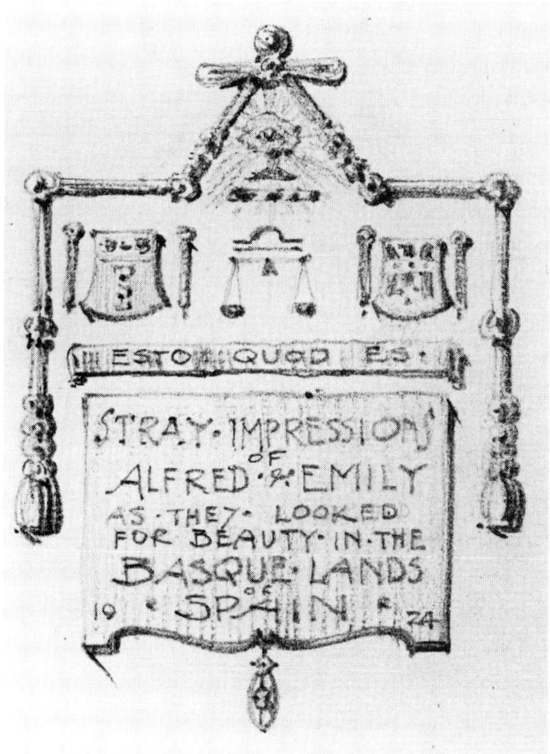

A recent photograph of a detail from one of a pair of lacquered chests designed by Alfred C. Bossom showing his Restoration of Fort Ticonderoga, 1908–25

A sketch from the Spanish drawings book: the Alcazar, Segovia.

'snap', and so became the owners of the most talked about piece of sculpture of the day. The story goes, that King George V sent a message saying how pleased he was that Bossom had bought it because now, he hoped, he could break it up! This he did not do but instead sent it around the country raising a great deal of money for various charities.

It would be a Herculean task to try and relate all my memories concerning my father's activities. I have only tried to show what an original, creative and forward thinking individual he was. For example, every year he painstakingly drew a topical Christmas card which he sent out in the form of a small architectural blueprint – a personal ritual he continued for over fifty years. He sculpted an eight-foot West Coast Indian style family totem pole and designed several pieces of family furniture, including two spectacular Chinese lacquer cabinets. On closer inspection these are seen to be decorated, not with dragons, but with his buildings and his beloved Mayan Temples, thus giving a pictorial relief of his American career.

In 1953 he was created a Baronet, and in 1959 was made one of the first Life Peers. The Heralds of the College of Arms were somewhat surprised when he designed for his Arms the representation of a steel building column, with three floor girders and appropriate wind bracing projections – this they had never seen. And for supporters he chose to have a Knight of the Shires of the time of King Charles I on one side, and a Green Mountain Boy of the American Revolutionary Force at Fort Ticonderoga on the other. Original, to say the least.

He died in 1965 at the age of eighty-four. Amazingly, he was still planning far ahead as there were so many things he was hoping to do and see. Somehow he never seemed to grow old, and this was well summed up by the grandchildren who, when they were quite young, once said 'Isn't Grandpa wonderful, he understands what we're talking about'.

He will always be vividly remembered by us, his family, and by his vast numbers of friends from all parts of his life and from many countries.

The Hon Sir Clive Bossom Bt., 1984 (Photo: Finlay).

Alfred Bossom's American Skyscrapers

Dennis Sharp and Peter Wylde

At the turn of the 20th century Alfred C Bossom was still studying for a career in architecture. A quarter of a century later he was one of the most successful commercial architects in New York. Even by American standards his success was sensational, if not unusual in a profession that was desperately trying to keep up with the needs of expanding business and burgeoning cities.

During the early part of his career Bossom was known as a bank architect responsible for a good number of tall buildings in new cities throughout the United States. Most of these were carried out in an architectural style that might be conveniently described as 'Bankers' classical'. During the latter period he was in the United States he assumed much more importance as a theorist and a prolific writer of articles on architectural topics, many of which pursued the high ideal of discovering a truly American architecture. That is, an architecture that was appropriate to the high buildings that were being erected everywhere in the United States in steel and concrete skeleton construction which demanded to be clothed in something more appropriate than European classical dress. Bossom's importance as an innovator of design ideas for a 'Modern American Architecture' should not be underestimated. Although his architectural vocabulary had ranged from a straightforward plagiarism of the Vitruvian McKim, Mead and White through a simplified structural phase, his enthusiasm for things Mayan and the impetus provided by the Paris Expo of 1925 placed him – in his last few buildings in the United States – as an important protagonist of the Art Deco skyscraper style of the late 1920s.[1]

Bossom's Early Career

The talent and energy which were to characterize Alfred Bossom's later career showed at a very early stage. Born in London on 16 October, 1881 he was educated at St Thomas Charterhouse School in the City where he won a number of scholarships and became head boy. He grew up in Islington. At the age of 16 and on the strength of his abilities he entered Regent St Polytechnic. It was there that he committed himself to an architectural career. During his period of training he travelled extensively on the Continent, won numerous medals, qualified as a carpenter and excelled in a bricklaying competition. In 1899 he commenced his career firstly as a draughtsman and later as an architect in the Housing Section of the London County Council. He became one of the youngest ever pupils at the Royal Academy Schools during this time. At the LCC he designed workers' cottages. At the Royal Academy he was later offered an invitation to go to the United States as an architect to design a housing scheme at Allegheny for the Carnegie Steel Mills Company, Pittsburgh. He gladly accepted the invitation from Andrew Carnegie's partner Henry Phipps and left for the USA at the end of 1903. He was to stay there until 1926 although during this period he was to travel extensively through Europe.[2]

The America which Bossom found on his arrival was a country still in the midst of hectic expansion and development. It had a population of 50 million in 1880 which in turn was doubled by 1913. Bossom arrived at the time of the explosive growth of cities in the South and Mid-West. The population had flocked to the cities on the rapidly expanding trans-continental railroads and within them expansion was helped by the electric street cars and the increasing demand for land. The wealth of these cities was generated by a raw and thriving capitalism: it was the era of the great corporations ruled over by business barons. Money was based on oil, banking, railroads, and new consumer products. Bossom wrote with admiration of the 'rugged, dominant steel-masters' and 'oil magnates' who were 'busily opening up the vast treasure-house of American wealth'. A good example was Samuel Bayne, an immigrant from Northern Ireland, who purchased America's second oil-well, in Titusville, Pennsylvania, and went on to establish his Seaboard Bank to deal in oil certificates. The spirit of the time is seen in the story of how Bayne, arriving in Dallas on the train, saw that the burgeoning city lacked a bank, and so organised one before departing on the next train

four hours later. Bossom married his daughter Emily in 1910; soon after his marriage he began to become known as a key bank architect and engineer. His first skyscraper job for Bayne was the Virginia Railway and Power Co Building, Richmond, Virginia, a 20-storey structure in the Classical style.

Architectural Practice

It was against the background of booming America that Bossom had begun to build up his practice in Pittsburgh. Although it seems that he had intended to stay in the United States for only a few months, he found the country's enterprising spirit congenial and decided to remain. Little is known of him in these early American years, except that after having completed the Pittsburgh housing he restored, in 1907 (the year he met Emily Bayne) the historic War of Independence Fort Ticonderoga at Lake Champlain in New York State. In doing so he became involved with the Pell family for whom he later built a residence in the Colonial style with a pseudo-Lutyens/Jekyll garden.

Bossom's success in this early period of his career came through his specialisation in the lucra-

The First National Bank of Richmond. Detail of cornice.

An aerial view showing the huge bulk of the new Magnolia Petroleum Co. Building in Dallas, Texas, 1922.

Magnolia Petroleum Co. Building, Dallas, Texas. The main entrance to the Banking Hall.

Main entrance of the Trenton Trust Co. building.

The Kanawha Valley Bank, Charleston, W.Va. Pencil drawing (1923) of the first scheme based on the Dallas Magnolia project.

Trenton Trust Company, New Jersey, 1924–25

The Banking Hall of the Trenton Trust Co. building. 1925.

The Kanawha Valley Bank, Charleston, W.Va. Perspective rendering showing the building in its final form 1923.

tive field of building for the banks, whose successes at that time can be measured by the great expansion of trade and boundaries. Help in building up his practice came from the architectural profession; Francis H Kimball as Bossom records in his book *Building to the Skies*, provided him with help in carrying out his first skyscraper project for the Chesapeake and Ohio Railway at Richmond, Va in 1910. A year later, in 1911, Bossom had established enough of a reputation to be invited to write a knowledgeable article in the national *Bankers' Magazine* on 'The Requirements of a Modern Bank Building'.[3] This article successfully gave the impression to potential clients that he had been building them for years. From then on banks remained the staple of his American architectural career, nearly all of them in the form of skyscrapers.

It was this building type that Bossom influenced in a notable way, and which then dominated American commercial building. The origins of the skyscraper lay in the new demand for central business premises and associated high land values. Admittedly Bossom did not invent the skyscraper but he did build on a number of occasions the first example of this new type of building in expanding cities such as Dallas, Texas, and Richmond, Virginia.

Skyscraper Construction

Bossom was working at a time when skyscraper construction had already reached maturity. He viewed the history of this building type as arising from a series of mutually complementary inventions the chief of which was skeleton construction.

This form of construction, he recognised, was developed by Chicago architects (Jenney's Home Insurance Co Building of 1884–85) but was eventually perfected in New York when Bessemer-produced steel supplanted the iron used in earlier structures. Constraint of height had been eliminated by the elevator and in particular the fast electric type was made possible by Roebling's development of the wire rope. Every invention contributed to the solution of further problems, eg Bossom's colleague Francis H Kimball greatly improved the foundations of skyscraper buildings by adopting the concrete caisson principle used in bridge construction and applying it to buildings in New York.

In the light of this it would seem that Bossom's greatest achievement as an architect in America was to implement existing techniques with the maximum efficiency rather than to innovate. Although he sub-titled his firm 'Bank Architect and Equipment Engineer' we do not know how much this implied in practice, apart from the fact that like all American firms he had to produce detailed con-

The Liberty Bank of Buffalo Building, Buffalo, NY. 1925. Construction photograph. Even during the most severe winter weather the progress of the building had to go on.

Perspective drawing showing the proposed Liberty Bank.

First National Bank of Jersey City, 1922.

structional drawings without the use of bills of quantities. He thoroughly mastered skyscraper construction and was fully aware of its revolutionary nature and potential. He waxed enthusiastic concerning foundations and refers in his book to the 'romantic spectacle' of excavating seven storeys with steam shovels and the sight of the pumping, piling and shoring of side walls, all of them a 'seven-league jump' from previous methods.[4] He emphasised that the erection of the steel frame at the rate of 4 storeys a week was, like all the elements of a skyscraper 'an assembling job' of 'innumerable component parts' which were necessarily factory-produced and standardised. He also saw clearly the two major implications of the use of the steel frame: that the outer wall became 'merely a façade for decorative effect' and could be of any material; and that the building's internal use and layout could be completely flexible: 'the most elastic type of building ever designed'. Equally important for Bossom was the careful planning of services, those arteries which ran through to the heart of the skyscraper itself. Here he again urged standardization, including one-pipe system plumbing and sophisticated mechanical ventilation to bring 'clean and exhilarating air' to every office worker. Bossom incorporated all these elements in his office buildings and combined them with a similarly thorough solution for a mass of other practical problems, eg those of fire safety and the security of bank vaults.

Bossom the practical manager saw the real key to success in his architectural practice as the elimination of delay, muddle and waste, a theme which is vigorously expressed all through *Building to the Skies* and of course in his Parliamentary career after he returned to England in 1926. He claimed that the building industry in the United States had already gone a long way towards adopting a 'corporate and co-operative' spirit amongst all the parties involved and, he argued, by adherence to a 'Time and Progress Schedule' – which he defines as the agreed plan of the whole work – there is 'allotted to each section of it a specific date for its (the work's) accomplishment'. When combined with the continual frank exchange of information between architects and contractors, this timetable became the inflexible basis for the operation with 'no idle men waiting for material and no material accumulating without the men to handle it'. In this unremitting 'campaign against time' work had to go on in all weathers, as it did for instance at the Liberty Bank, Buffalo, built between 1924–25, where tarpaulins and braziers protected the workmen against freezing cold. This building, costing about £1m in those days, demonstrated the success of the methods used. It was built in 333 days, which was significantly less than the originally agreed contract period.

The Art of the Skyscraper

However, skyscrapers had another aspect: as Bossom wrote, they were also 'placards of prosperity and success', built as the finest form of self-expression and advertisement by the companies whose names they bore, objects of intense local pride and rivalry in their respective cities. In New York successive buildings were each briefly renowned as the greatest structure yet: from the Flatiron Building of 1902 through the Singer Building of 1908, said to have paid for itself by extra sales of sewing-machines within a year, to the Metropolitan Life Insurance Building of 1909.

In his book *Delirious New York* Rem Koolhaas traces the uncertain evolution of these buildings between a 'block' and a 'tower' form leading to a synthesis in the Woolworth Building of 1913, which was built to advertise the financial stability of the 'five-and-ten-cent' stores.[5] At 792 feet high, this was the tallest of all. It was christened the 'Cathedral of Commerce' and seen as the defini-

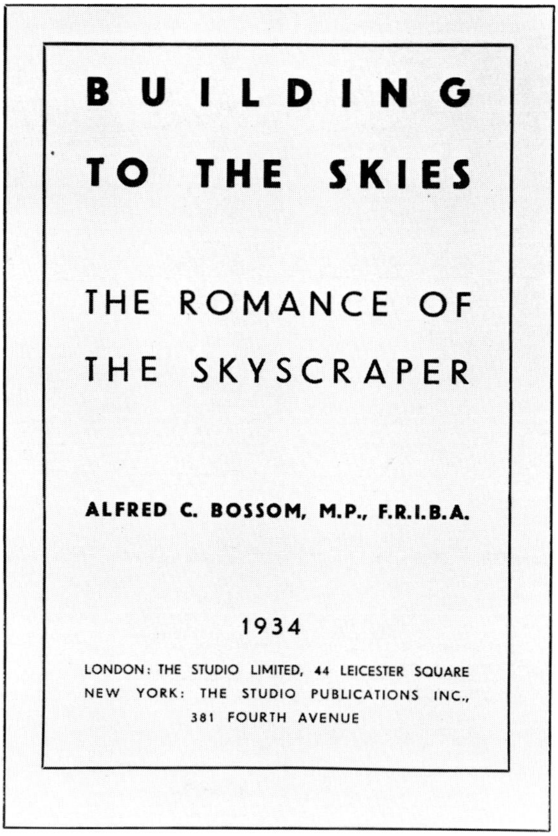

BUILDING TO THE SKIES

THE ROMANCE OF THE SKYSCRAPER

ALFRED C. BOSSOM, M.P., F.R.I.B.A.

1934

LONDON: THE STUDIO LIMITED, 44 LEICESTER SQUARE
NEW YORK: THE STUDIO PUBLICATIONS INC., 381 FOURTH AVENUE

tive skyscraper. It evoked lyrical praise. Bossom wrote: 'It is thoroughly American in its utilisation of space, in its convenience, in its engineering, and certainly it is one of the many monuments to American achievement. It is well ornamented, even lavishly, but still it is American.[6] Bossom had begun, like many other emigrés, to search for the Holy Grail of American 'democratic' architecture.

His search began with what he regarded as the first valid, or earliest American style, the neo-Renaissance of McKim, Mead & White. In 1924 Lewis Mumford labelled this the 'Imperial Age' in American architecture, and showed how appropriate this grand Roman manner Stanford White and others practised was for the 'imperial men' – the business magnates who ruled American life. In

DEVELOPING THE ENVELOPE

Preliminary drawings to determine a form for a maximum sized building permissible on a site.

New York classicism had become the established norm and was used to clothe the skyscrapers by means of likening them to a single classical column, setting up a three-part division into base, shaft, and crowning feature. Many of the lesser McKim, Mead & White buildings used this scheme, often with simple fenestration and a heavily-loaded cornice, and these Bossom must have taken as his model. For instance McKim, Mead & White's Munsey Building in Baltimore, 1908–13, is echoed in Bossom's design for the First National Bank, Jersey City of 1921. In *Building to the Skies* he illustrates and acknowledges his debt to their Gorham Building in New York of 1903–06.

Bossom was also led towards classicism by virtue of his specialisation in banks for which it was regarded as especially suitable. The external appearance of a bank was a crucial means of attracting would-be depositors, and in the *Banker's Magazine* article Bossom stresses that 'this should be made inviting to convey the desired impression of conservative enterprise, which alone will inspire confidence'.[7] In design and materials 'the most important requirement is that the building shall be devoid of anything appearing tawdry, vulgar or cheap'. Inevitably then he fell back on a sober classicism. He was commended for this in a magazine review of his Seaboard National Bank in 1922, where as the writer said, 'none but the radically-minded will deplore this'.[8]

Bossom's architectural philosophy was frankly honest, perhaps naively so, but it clearly related architectural integrity to quality of materials. He wrote: 'Every layman now knows that the old-fashioned system of decorating the windows with large iron pipes to imitate impregnable protection is a pure fake . . . The best quality of granite, marble, limestone, brick, etc., should be used to create an eminently substantial looking building if the whole be treated with skill. Anything of a perishable nature should under no circumstances be used, for such materials as zinc, tin, etc., soon present a dilapidated appearance and thus indicate that poor taste has been employed in the construction of the building (sic). This does not tend to inspire confidence in the bank's judgement in other matters that concerns its customers . . . Solidity cannot be too strongly impressed upon the outside of the building.'[9]

Such 'solidity' decked out in classical forms is well seen in Bossom's major buildings, which share a common character. Typically their form was based on rectangular blocks or a combination of blocks which did not disguise their basic frame. This 'feeling' was brought out in the pencil sketch for the Trenton Trust Company Building of c1924. Classical detail, as in the street frontage of the same building, was in low relief. It was correct and chaste, even delicate. Bossom could err towards extravagance such as the pilastered tower of the Hibernia Bank, New Orleans, which is used to support a strange tempietto in the sky. But the best of his buildings show a simple elegance which relies on plain masses and worthwhile materials: the 14 floors of buff-coloured brickwork on the Liberty Bank of Buffalo rise uninterrupted above the granite and limestone-clad base.

Besides the conviction that neo-Classicism was the right and proper means of expression of a civic and dignified architecture of the city Bossom continued to seek an apposite 'American' idiom. Of this national style he wrote that it 'is of the soil, the air and the customs of a century . . . It springs from the needs of a race. It is a portrait in stone of the type of life lived . . .' It is to be observed, Bossom argued, that 'there were on this continent . . . long before Columbus, people who were much the same horizon of culture as the archaic Greeks. If Mound

Trenton Trust Co., Trenton, NJ. 1924–25. Perspective drawing of the first scheme for the new bank.

Preliminary studies, giving what is known as the envelope, beyond which the structure cannot legally project, by Harvey Corbett and Hugh Ferris. Thus a form for a maximum sized building on a site is determined.

Buildings, Mayas, Toltecs, Aztecs, the subjects of the Incas, had not been put out of their stride by certain Europeans . . .' a fine civilisation would have developed.[10] In *Building to the Skies* Bossom gives these earlier thoughts almost symphonic meaning. He enlarges his score: 'It is almost a law of architectural necessity that the Americans in stretching their buildings skywards should come to the same treatments of flat surfaces, set-backs and ornamented silhouettes.' The analogy here is to the famous complex of temples of Tikal in Guatemala, the chief of which built in AD 770 adds up in Bossom's estimation, to the 'original American skyscraper'.[11] This argument was certainly shared by members of the Architectural League of New York in the mid-twenties (when Bossom acted as Treasurer). The 41st Annual Exhibition in 1926 indicated at least one monumental reconstruction by Helmle and Corbett in a vaguely American (in this case Hollywood American and pseudo-Maya – or perhaps, Babylonian revival style). By some sort of international coincidence it was induced, if not born, of the Paris Exposition of 1925 after which this pseudo-Mayan type had its moment of glory as an acquired American idiom. Bossom's somewhat imaginative summary of its manifestations among East coasters was its swan-song.

This drawing represents a reconstruction of the largest of the temples (AD 770) at Tikal, Guatemala, which Alfred Bossom considered the archetypal American skyscraper.

On Leaving America

Bossom's departure from the US in late 1926, although clearly well considered, was nevertheless somewhat abrupt. It occurred at the height of his professional career and during the boom years of New York's upward building expansion. Perhaps he well knew – as any banker's architect probably would – that the slump was just around the corner although he later explained that '. . . the magnet of home seemed to pull us irresistably . . . away from New York with its skyscrapers, back to England'.[12] In the event he returned to a country still feeling the effects of a crippling General Strike. Whilst he continued for some time to act as a consultant for American projects he 'began a new life entirely detached' from his practice as an architect.[13] Meanwhile he settled temporarily in Mayfair before moving to St James's.

When he left America his most articulate 'Art Deco' or 'National Style' skyscraper, the Petroleum Building in Houston, Texas, was still not complete. He left too before there was any practical opportunity to construct the appropriate 'recessional' edifice he so eloquently illustrated and wrote of in an article in *The Spur* magazine in August 1926.[14]

Bossom's unfulfilled American career leaves much to the imagination. Would this tirelessly energetic and well educated English architect really have made an indelible mark in the development of a 'native' and truly indigenous American architecture? It is perhaps a gratuitous question but nevertheless one worth posing in relation to his interest – along with his colleagues Corbett, Ferris and others – in finding a tall, commercial and yet expressive architecture capable of conveying more than a monetary message and a momentary symbolic gesture. That was left to Frank Lloyd Wright who more than anyone else brought the Mayan Revival and Art Deco to life and created a truly American democratic architecture. During the period after he visited the Paris Exposition of 1925 Bossom appears to have received enough inspiration to re-evaluate his views of a modern, native architecture for North America. The trip provided him with the fillip necessary to engage in an entirely new approach to design that eschewed the pseudo-stylistic and the Beaux Arts.

It surprised him that the Americans had produced nothing of significance themselves for the Paris World Exposition.[15] Paris however provided an invaluable incentive to Bossom's own imagination. When combined with the aspects of Mayan architecture he admired, the forms used by the Paris *Expo* designers could be imaginatively blown up in scale to fit the expressive needs of commercial skyscraper design. In a sense the acceptance of this new expressive language (perhaps nowhere better displayed than in the Rockefeller Complex off Fifth Avenue some years later) replaced his previous allegiance to classicism. The Houston Petroleum Building, which was being designed at this time (summer 1925) was the first example of his new attitude. Bossom with this project claimed that he wanted to do 'something different' in order to make it '101 per cent American' both in overall massing and in decorative detail.[16]

In a way Parisian Art Deco forms provided an inspirational source for the skin that went over the skeleton of his skyscraper structures. The arguments he put forward for 'recessional towers' in his *Spur* article emphasise the need to shape the envelope. The recessions themselves – now rationalized along horizontal lines – were based on setbacks allowed for in US zoning laws. In fact he probably saw these parts of the skyscrapers as a series of pavilions which when combined made up a complete block: 'The Paris pavilions', he wrote in his review of the 1925 Expo, '. . . have an air of height which has been obtained by the skillful handling of the horizontal.'[17] The previous paragraph had extolled the vertical which he found: '. . . dominant everywhere. Here are straight lines and forms in seemingly endless repetition. Long upright lines rush upward in that heaven-daring spirit which marks the architecture of the ancient Mayans – and that which we see in some of our modern architecture in this country, where skyscrapers stand like Titans with their heads in the sky'.[18] Later he claimed that the emphatic vertical expression of commercial building was 'uniquely American'. During a further trip to Europe in 1926 when he spent some time in Germany as the guest of the *Bund Deutscher Architekten* he was able to observe at first hand the Hamburg Expressionists' use of vertical brickwork design.[19]

The Mayan Interest seems to have been originally fuelled by a trip he and his wife had taken to Central America in 1921. Some of the sketches from this and subsequent tours were published in his lavish book *An Architectural Pilgrimage in Old Mexico* of 1924. They bear testimony to the consistency of his search for an indigenous American architecture which had roots in earlier civilisations in that part of the Continent. His own imaginative projects, published in *Building to the Skies* were based on his reconstruction drawings (in turn based on those of George Oakley Totten) of the major Tikal Temple in Guatemala.[20] From this model his most mature New York Madison Avenue Project emerged.[21]

The Petroleum Building at Houston, Texas, 1925–26

Skyscraper Project in the 'recessed' style, Madison Ave, New York, c1925

A Second Career

The choice of a second career in public and political service eventually took Bossom away from architectural practice but never far from architecture and building. He remained a perceptive critic of both fashions and methods of the constructional business world writing articles in numerous journals.

He acted on many institutional boards, sponsored developments in the arts – including securing the safety of Jacob Epstein's sculpture 'Genesis' – and probably most importantly served as a key 'expert' on Lord Portal's Mission on 'prefabricated' housing methods.[22] This entailed a lengthy return trip to the USA in 1943 during which time he observed the effects of mechanisation on house design and in particular how it influenced the production of the two-part transportable 'prefabs' erected by the Tenessee Valley Authority.[23] However, although he still occasionally designed, and never really lost his keen interest in drawing, Bossom's mature influence became more subtly pervasive. To this day the institutions he believed in and helped still use his name to honour their more distinguished speakers or students.

References

1 The Spanish and Mayan aspects of the Art Deco Style are probably displayed best in buildings on the west coast of the USA. These influences have been well documented by Professor David Gebhard of the University of California, Santa Barbara, whose two publications, *The Richfield Building, 1928–68*, Los Angeles 1970, and *Kem Weber*, Santa Barbara 1969 show the richness of this applied tradition. A more general account of the development (including a brief reference to Bossom's contribution to it) may be found in Hillier, B (Ed) *The World of Art Deco*, Minneapolis and London, 1971.
A less known indication of the application of Art Deco motifs to skyscraper buildings, particularly of those in the 'futuristic' mould, are to be found in the pages of the *Encyclopaedia Britannica*, 14th edn (1929) under the section heading 'Architecture', edited by H. W. Corbett the drawings for this section were prepared by Bossom's colleagues Hugh Ferris, Cass Gilbert and Helmle Corbett.
For a study of the New York Art Deco Skyscraper see Cervin Robinson and Rosemarie Haag Bletter, *Skyscraper Style: Art Deco New York*, New York: OUP 1975 and in particular the essay written by Dr Bletter on 'The Art Deco Style' pp 35–81.

2 In the sources and documents section of this publication part of a previously unpublished autobiography is included. It outlines Bossom's earlier education and records his original invitation to the United States.

3 Alfred C Bossom, 'The Requirements of a Modern Bank Building', in *The Bankers Magazine*, New York, Nov 1911, Vol 83 pp 658–62.

4 Alfred C Bossom, *Building to the Skies*, London and New York: The Studio, 1934, pp 76, 85–86.

5 Rem Koolhaas, *Delirious New York*, London: Thames & Hudson, 1978.

6 Alfred C Bossom, 'Fifty Years' Progress Toward an American Style in Architecture', *American Architect*, Jan 5, 1926, p 48.

7 Bossom, 'The Requirements . . .', *Op Cit*.

8 M Price, 'The Seaboard National Bank, New York City', *Architectural Record*, May 1922, p 478.

9 Bossom, 'The Requirements . . .', *Op Cit*.

10 Bossom, 'Fifty Years' Progress . . .', *Op Cit*, p 48

11 *Building to the Skies*, *Op Cit*, p 18.

12 From *Bossom Family Christmas Cards 1915 to 1947*, London 1948, for private circulation. 1926.

13 *Ibid*.

14 Alfred C Bossom, 'The "Recessional" Building', *The Spur*, New York, August 1926, p 41.

15 Alfred C Bossom, 'The Rebirth of Art and Architecture in Europe', *American Architect*, Vol 128, No 2479, Aug 26, 1925 pp 161–6.

16 From report: 'American Motifs . . .' in *Houston Post Dispatch*, Dec 16, 1925.

17 Bossom, 'The Rebirth of Art . . .', *Op Cit*.

18 *Ibid*.

19 Alfred C Bossom, 'Verticality in Design as Expressed in the Work of German Architects', *American Architect*, Vol 131, No 2513, Jan 20, 1927, pp 63–70.

20 George Oakley Totton, *Maya Architecture*, Washington DC: Maya Press, 1926. See item on Tikal, pp 52–3.

21 This photograph was widely shown in American Publications, It was later re-used in *Building to the Skies* and appears to be one of two views that were made for the proposed office project. As far as it can be ascertained the project was never built and there is no indication that a client was involved.

22 An interesting comment is made on Bossom's purchase of 'Genesis' in Charles Reilly's *Scaffolding in the Skies*, London, 1938.

23 Published as a Government Mission Report, *Methods of Building in the USA*, London: HMSO, 1944.

Alfred Charles Bossom: Specialist in Bank Design

Martha B Caldwell
James Madison University

From his design of the First National Bank of Richmond, Virginia (1910) to that of the Liberty Bank of Buffalo, New York (1924), Alfred Charles Bossom graced the towns and cities of America with ornate and dignified houses of finance. His initial commissions were in Virginia and North Carolina, but after a hiatus in his architectural work during the years of World War I, Bossom designed banks in the New York area, as well as other states until 1926. Following norms of the time, these structures were eclectic in design using motifs drawn largely from ancient, Renaissance and 16th century architecture. In the 1920s, however, first in his writing and later in his architecture, he developed new ideas and moved away from reliance on European prototypes towards a style which suggests Art Deco.

Bossom's architectural specialty in banks may have come about through family connections. In 1910 he married Emily Bayne whose father, Samuel Bayne, a native of Northern Ireland, purchased the second oil well drilled in the United States near Titusville, Pennsylvania. He organised oil distribution and established the Seaboard Bank to deal in oil certificates. It may be assumed that Bayne made his son-in-law known to bankers. Certainly, Bossom's determination to be a specialist in bank design is shown by an article published in 1911 in *The Bankers Magazine* entitled 'The Requirements of a Modern Bank Building.'[1] Illustrating the article with a drawing of the future First National Bank in Richmond – his only commission at that time which involved banking – Bossom engaged in some subdued self-advertising:

'. . . one who has made a special study of the entire banking question as applied to its home, and who would not allow one consideration to have undue prominence to the disadvantage of another, can aid indefinitely in installing the bank in quarters that will be both economical and efficient in its conduct . . .'.[2]

Late 19th and early 20th century architects in America, including Bossom made extensive use of source books of European architecture and details. High-rise structures generally had three parts to their elevations, a format which can be traced to H H Richardson and the early skyscrapers of Chicago. Perusal of work by contemporaries of Bossom, such as Francis Kimball, Carriere and Hastings, E R Graham, Clinton and Russell, and McKim, Mead and White indicates that all share general similarities. The closest to Bossom's designs was the Gorham Building in New York by Charles F McKim; Bossom himself presented this comparison in *Building to the Skies*.[3] The Gorham Build-

First National Bank, Richmond, Virginia, 1912–13

ing, like the First National Bank in Richmond and the First National Bank in Jersey City, had attached half columns at the top.

In the above cited article in *The Bankers Magazine*, Bossom presented some design ideas: 'The building externally should be distinctive, should look like a BANK and should call attention to itself by its substantial and conservative appearance'.[4] In a later article, also in *The Bankers Magazine*, Bossom writes of the importance of doorways as latent advertising for the bank, and notes that 'the Old World is ransacked for suggestions and ideas and the more interesting and distinctive these are the greater become their desirability'.[5] Bossom's 'Old World' sources vary but he showed a predilection for Italian Renaissance forms. Writing in 1921 Bossom noted:
'The Italian Renaissance was a radical, modern expression of the forward life of the time, yet it wrought in the rediscovered art forms of the classic past. It was the spirit of its own time which made it intrinsically great, but the perfected traditional art forms which it employed lent sureness and serenity to its expression.'[6] Bossom turned also to the work of 16th century architects; for example the Villa Madama near Rome by Giulio Romano and Giovanni Udine was the source for detailing in the Greenwich (Conn) Trust Company of the early 1920s.[7] Greek and Roman architecture was a source as well. The Merchant's Bank in Durham, North Carolina, had Ionic columns, pilasters and mouldings like those found on the Erechtheum in Athens, and the Virginia Trust Company's entrance arch and inside detailing reminds us of Roman prototypes.

Great Neck Trust Company, Long Island, 1925

Liberty Bank of Buffalo, 1924–25

Interiors of Bossom's banks were largely given over to large banking rooms richly built with various marbles and granites. Generally the space was lit with large windows and with decorative chandeliers. Metalwork, generally bronze, graced the windows, doors and tellers' cages. The banking rooms usually featured an officers' section separated by a railing or on a raised platform.[8] In some of the early banks Bossom provided women with separate spaces screened from general public view.[9] Oak, walnut or mahogany panels enriched board rooms and office spaces. Cast metal or stone carvings of winged figures with floral spirals were a motif Bossom used as decoration on walls, flanking clocks, or above doorways in several banks including the Virginia Trust Company, the Trenton Trust Company and the Jersey City First National Bank.

Ornamentation on a Bossom-designed building should be carefully observed, for he was highly inventive and at times very romantic. We find nude nymphs on Richmond's First National Bank, labradors in the roundels on the Virginia Trust Company next door,[10] and 'flashing beacons of amity' borne by replicas of the Statue of Liberty in

Hibernia Bank at New Orleans, 1920–21

Metal Bank vaults for the Hibernia

Buffalo.[11] Surely the most interesting decorations were on the Virginia Electric and Power Company in Richmond. As built in 1915, the VEPCO Building had a popular roof garden surrounded by a parapet. Standards on the parapet discharged high pressure steam on which red lights played, giving the appearance of flaming braziers. Above the lower entablature, Bossom placed a row of hooded electric light posts.[2] The building was indeed decorated in a highly dramatic and appropriate manner.

In overall design, we can observe a tendency toward bolder forms. For example, if one compares the 1911 First National Bank in Richmond, with the 1924 Trenton Trust Company, this tendency is apparent at a glance. The single bold entrance arch of the Trenton Trust Company, the unbroken rise of floors, and the comparatively simplified top section differs from the more busily decorated First National Bank. To see this bolder tendency one need look no further than next door to the First National Bank – at the Virginia Trust Company. The great Roman arch of the Virginia Trust Company, rising four floors in height, is one of the most beautiful landmarks of Richmond. As Fiske Kimball wrote: 'Few banks anywhere achieve greater dignity than the Virginia Trust Company in Richmond.'[13] We are fortunate to have the two structures side by side enabling us to see Bossom as designer of both skyscraper and 'temple-like' banks at the same time.

The First National Bank in Richmond was Bossom's first bank design, his first skyscraper, and the first skyscraper in the South. In writings about the building an idea is found which Bossom stressed throughout his career – the idea of 'time and progress'. Bossom believed in careful scheduling of the progress of the construction so men and materials would be available when needed and in order that the client would be able to move in on the day specified. Bossom described the 'time and progress' of this building, noting that it had to be completed in nine months:

'It took a little over three months to put down the foundations which were dug by hand by open cut method nearly 80 feet into the ground. I can assure you that I almost got housemaid's knees praying that none of the shoring would give way in the holes while the men were digging. Less than six months after the foundations were finished, that 250 feet building was completed and the railway moved in on the appointed day.

Such a performance would have been impossible had it not been known in advance where everything was coming from and on what date, and in what quantities, and where to put it and what to do with it on arrival.'[14]

Virginia Trust Company, Richmond, Virginia, 1919–20

First National Bank, Richmond, Va.

The First National Bank of Richmond, Va.

Bossom in the South

Bossom contributed significantly to Southern architecture in the USA. Fiske Kimball, in a 1924 survey of architecture in the South, singled out Bossom's Magnolia Building and various bank buildings for discussion. It is apparent that Kimball recognised Bossom's importance to the history of architecture in the South.[15] In Virginia, his early bank commissions were in both the capital city and in the western part of the state. The First National Bank of Richmond was built in 1912–13. In 1914 he remodelled the interior of the First National Bank of Lexington. In 1915–16 he designed the Lynchburg National Bank with its palatial interior, great windows and stained glass dome. The People's Bank in Harrisonburg (1916), now the Rockingham County Office Building, complements the earlier Richardsonian buildings on Court Square in a truly commendable way. Two banks were designed for the western Virginia community of Covington: the Covington National Bank, begun prior to World War I and finished in 1918 and the Citizens National Bank of 1919. Bossom also designed at least three apartment buildings in Virginia, two in Richmond and one in Lynchburg, and helped to select the architect for Richmond's Municipal Building.[16]

In North Carolina, after a fire burned out the centre of Durham in 1914, Bossom designed two very different banks. The Fidelity Bank (Geer Building), five storeys high, was derived from a Florentine palazzo. A half block away, the Merchant's Bank had Greek Ionic elements. Greek sources also were used for the Charlotte National Bank where Doric columns and entablature give a sense of severity to this Bossom building. A skyscraper, still the tallest building in Wayne County, was put up in Goldsboro in 1923–24 to house the Wayne National Bank.

Dallas, Texas was the site of Bossom's most important skyscraper, the Magnolia Building of 1922 (now the Mobil Building), the tallest structure in the South for a number of years. Preceding the Magnolia in Dallas was a high-rise bank built in 1918 – the American Exchange National Bank. Designed in association with the local firm of Lang and Witchell, this nineteen-storey structure attracted much attention as it was built. 'Crowds would gather each day to watch the workmen because it was the most imposing building of its time.'[17] Like all Bossom designs, the interior had excellent metal work. 'It took one employee full time to polish the cages and doors to a mirror shine.'[18]

Elsewhere in the South, Bossom contributed to a major skyscraper in Louisiana. The Hibernia Bank in New Orleans (1920–21), seems to have been largely designed by a local firm, Favrot and

Magnolia Petroleum Building at Dallas, Texas, 1922

The Hibernia Bank & Trust Co., New Orleans, as constructed 1921.

The People's Bank at Harrisonburg, Virginia, 1916

Livaudis, but Bossom was commissioned to design an imposing interior and evidently to help with technical problems. Bossom wrote that he had 'a most interesting experience in New Orleans':

'I was asked by the Hibernia Bank if they could have a building twice the height of anything in Louisiana. New Orleans stands in the delta of the Mississippi. I have always had a theory that no delta existed naturally and that at some time there must have been some solid layer upon which the silt could pile up, otherwise it would have simply been an arm of the sea.

'With a contractor, a pile-driving machine and two 60-foot wood piles, we went to an open lot and drove the first. It went down several feet at each blow until about fifty feet in the ground; then it stopped almost dead. From that point on the driving was slow, but after about eight feet more, one blow, and the pile shot into the ground out of sight. The pile-driving machine was moved to another spot and the same thing happened to the second pile. This proved that at a level of about fifty feet beneath there was something solid.

'An auger was obtained. This forces to the

surface the matter through which it passes, and we found at a level of about fifty-two feet below the city a layer of prehistoric oyster shells about eight feet thick which apparently had never been discovered before. With this information I went back to the bank and told them we could build practically anything as we had the desired solid base to start from.'[19]

The twenty-three storey building which was built remains a dominant landmark of New Orleans. The banking room, designed by Bossom, was surrounded by imposing Corinthian columns and great arched windows. The tellers' cages had metal grilles decorated with ancient and modern coin replicas. The raised platform for the officers of the bank was a continuing part of Bossom's banks. The exterior of the Hibernia Bank was presumably done by the local architects. The tempietto at the top seems a more delicate motif than we associate with Bossom. It is very close to the design by George Kendall, of McKim, Mead and White, for New York's Municipal Building.

Bossom's Northern Banks

Turning north, two high-rise banks, both of which are still in use and well maintained, can be found in New Jersey. The Trenton Trust Company, now the National State Bank, was designed in 1923 with an imposing arched entry including fine metal elements. Arched windows and a richly detailed coffered ceiling were the dominant features of the interior. Favourite Bossom ornaments, rosettes, winged figures with floral spirals and roundels (with heads?) were among the decorative features. Outside were cartouches that tell the story of the city's industries.[20]

The First National Bank, now the First Jersey National Corporation, in Jersey City, was designed in 1920 with a strong, compact vertical shape. Tall windows and attached columns at the top emphasized the rectangle as the dominant design element. Interior ornamentation in the large banking room, 100 by 80 feet, was strongly reminiscent of Palladio; the familiar winged figures with their floral spirals crown a Palladian-type doorway. However, the entrance to the bank had a white metal screen based upon the Caballeros in Cuenca Cathedral in Spain.[21]

Perhaps Bossom's most important bank design was the Seaboard National Bank on the corner of Beaver and Broad Street in the heart of New York's financial district. The Seaboard Bank later became a part of the Chase Manhattan Bank of New York, and this building was torn down in the mid-1950s to make room for a high-rise structure. However, in 1921 Bossom's beautifully detailed building received an award from the

First National Bank of Jersey City, 1922.

Downtown League for being the best building designed in 1921. The site of this old section of New York was a difficult one, but Bossom's solution with its angled plan and imposing flight of stairs to the main banking space was imaginative and effective. Symmetry was suggested despite an irregularly shaped layout. Polished granite Corinthian columns lining the street gave great dignity to this structure. The capital of each column had a representative seaboard animal worked into the design. Throughout the bank American materials were used, and in the entrance hall were reliefs of American heroes – Paul Revere and Sergeant York.[22]

The Liberty Bank Building in Buffalo, New York opened its doors on October 13, 1925. The familiar Renaissance decorative elements were employed in the detailing of the wall surfaces and in the interior decoration. However, Bossom was becoming dissatisfied with this sort of work. He stated that overall design of American skyscrapers was fine, but he added 'the speed with which these are needed due to the great interest charges and anxiety on the part of the owners to start the flow of income into their own pockets, have compelled the architects to use reference books *ad nauseam*.'[23] Bossom moved away from eclectic ornamentation in the last building he did in America, the

Seaboard National Bank, New York, 1920–21

Liberty Bank of Buffalo, NY, 1924–5
Sketch showing the masts and antennae of the Broadcasting Station in its right hand tower.

Petroleum Building in Houston, and in other projects drawn but not built.[24] In the Liberty Bank Building the beginnings of new design ideas based on the use of Pre-Columbian motifs and on a greater emphasis on the vertical and on colour were initiated.

On the roof of the Liberty Bank statues held lamps, 'flashing beacons of amity', which could be seen for a ten mile radius, including of course, Canada. The statues, done by Leo Lentelli, derive from Bartholdi's 'Statue of Liberty'.

'High and dry above Main Street, the twin matrons form a distinctive, if slightly fantastic feature of the Buffalo skyline. Facing east and west, they are prime symbols in the inconography of Buffalo as a city with a strategic national position. Indeed Bossom may have remembered that Bartholdi originally envisioned his colossus at the mouth of the Suez Canal, where it was to have marked an international coming together of far-flung civilizations.'[25]

The support for these two statues were pyramids whose source, according to Bossom, was Mayan architecture.[26] Travelling and writing in the mid 1920s, Bossom developed the belief that design motifs suitable for skyscraper construction could be found in Pre-Columbian architecture. Proper decoration for the distinctive American skyscraper should be that which was 'native American' – Mayan.[27] Undoubtedly, part of the reason for this decision lay in the 1916 zoning law of New York City, which set a formula resulting in setbacks; the tall slabs were no longer permitted. The stepped nature of pyramids, such as those at Tikal, resembled the setback blocks designed for New York.[28]

Colour in architecture is another topic Bossom stressed in his writing, although he used very subdued colour for the Liberty design, grey and light cream. 'The strongholds of security at the top recall in their hue the Eastern Legend of the Ivory Towers.'[29] As early as 1921 he wrote:

'America has outgrown "white architecture" and reached a period of artistic evolution wherein colour is a vital element in every complete architectural scheme. The signs of this are everywhere and the quality and scope of colour conceptions are daily enlarging.'[30] Bossom found signs of this not only in America but also later at the Paris International Exposition. In a survey of the exposition, he noted the various colour schemes, the remarkable and original lighting effects and the dominance of the vertical.[31]

The vertical in design Bossom found in both contemporary and earlier architecture of the Hanseatic League. Helping to arrange a 1927 exhibit collected by the German Foreign Office,

Newspaper cutting showing the perspective drawing of the Petroleum Building, Houston, Texas.

Bossom had the opportunity to study contemporary brick architecture in such German cities as Hamburg, Bremen and Lübeck. He believed American skyscraper designers could learn from the German work such as the *Chile Haus* Office Building and *Ballin Haus* in Hamburg.[32]

The ideas Bossom developed during the early and mid 1920s, the use of Pre-Columbian motifs, and emphasis on the vertical and on colour, were hallmark characteristics of Art Deco. Bossom, a

ARE WE AT THE DAWN OF A GREAT PEACE
ACB
MAY THE NEED FOR ARMIES AND NAVIES FADE AWAY
LET THIS BE OUR FIRST WISH FOR 1922
ALL THE SEASONS HAPPINESS
MR MRS ALFRED C BOSSOM
21 EAST 82ST NY CITY

Project for a World War Memorial, 1921

person of influence in New York,[33] and a prolific writer played a role in the development of this distinctive style. He was one of the first architects to recognise the merits of Art Deco. When asked to choose an exhibit in 1925 of American architecture for Berlin, Bossom and his colleague, Harvey Wiley Corbett, selected, among other buildings of quite traditional design, two buildings the Barclay-Vesey Building and the Insurance Center – both Art Deco.[34]

Bossom's unique qualities lay in the substantial and imposing aura of his buildings, in his use of highly inventive ornamentation, and in his choice of the best materials available. He must be admired for his use of the accepted and the traditional, as well as for his willingness and ability to explore new ideas and forms. His 'temple-like' banks and his skyscrapers were fine contributions to American architecture. The latter were especially important. Bossom began his major book, *Building To The Skies*, with the following passage:

'One can hardly think of America apart from skyscrapers and one cannot think at all of skyscrapers apart from America. They are the first stunning fact that confronts the traveller as he approaches New York and their lights, twinkling perhaps a thousand feet up in the sky, are often his last glimpse of land when he sails for Europe.

'Passing from city to city throughout the Union he never gets away from their dominant immensity, nor from the ceaselessly bubbling pride and interest that the citizens take in them. He soon comes to accept the skyscraper as America's most popular, as it is her most distinctive, contribution to architecture – perhaps her greatest permanent contribution to any of the arts.'[35]

Though the skyscraper is identified as an uniquely American art form, it was an Englishman who built some of the very best examples in the United States. Because banks are universally required structures, hamlets and great cities in America were the happy recipients of beautiful and imaginatively ornamented buildings designed by Alfred Charles Bossom.

References

1. Bossom, Alfred Charles (ACB), 'The Requirements of a Modern Bank Building', *The Bankers Magazine* 83, (Nov 1911) p 658ff
2. Ibid p 662
3. ACB, *Building To The Skies: The Romance of The Skyscraper* p 29; see also *American Arch* 129 (Jan 5, 1926) p 47
4. ACB, 'The Requirements . . .' *Op Cit* p 658
5. ACB, 'The Bank Doorway', *The Bankers Magazine* 99 (July–Dec 1919), p 74
6. ACB, 'Nicholas K. Roerich: His Art and Its Bearing on Mural Decoration in America', *Architectural Record*. L, No 2 (Aug 1921) p 92
7. *Architects' Journal* 56 (Oct 4, 1922) p 444
8. Today the tendency is to make the bank inviting, bright and cheerful and anything that will tend to make the customers more at home should be adopted. In institutions where the policy is to have as many patrons as possible known to the officers, the officers should be prominently located in the banking room and with only sufficient suggested privacy, contrived by interposing a low rail in front of their space, to prevent a waste of time by having to take part in unnecessary conversation. ACB, 'Requirements . . .', *Op Cit* p 659
9. Ladies' accounts have now become of such importance that special provision is made for miladi's comfort in all up-to-date banking establishments. Private rooms fitted with toilet articles, writing materials, mirrors and a 'stocking rail', and also tellers' wickets for their exclusive use, are an essential part of the modern bank's equipment. A good arrangement is to provide a small private room near the entrance to the bank and also to have an alcove between the tellers' cages provided with a curtain, enabling the same tellers to attend to the ladies without practically moving from their places. ACB, 'Requirements . . .', *Op Cit* pp 659–60
10. Robert Winthrop, *Architecture in Downtown Richmond*, p 170 and p 171 and *Cast and Wrought Metal*, p 108 and p 109
11. ACB, 'Twin Beacons of Amity', *American Arch* 129 (Jan 20, 1926) p 177ff
12. ACB, *Building To The Skies*, p 30
13. Fiske Kimball, 'Recent Architecture in the South', *Architectural Record* 55, No 3 (March 1924) p 229
14. ACB, *Building To The Skies*, pp 119–120
15. Kimball, *Op Cit* p 229ff
16. *Report of advisory architect on designs submitted in the competition for the selection of an architect and the procuring of a design for the proposed new municipal building*. Richmond, William Byrd Press, 1914
17. Field, Bobbi, *A History of the Metropolitan Savings and Loan Building*, Dallas, Texas (Privately Printed) 1977
18. Ibid
19. ACB, 'American Architecture', *Journal of the Royal Society of Arts*, (June 8, 1928) pp 779–80
20. ACB, Trenton Trust Company, *Bankers Magazine: Portfolio* 109 (July–Dec 1924) (Supplement)
21. ACB, 'New Home for the First National Bank, Jersey City', *Bankers Magazine* 105 (August 1922) p 486
22. ACB, 'New Home for the Seaboard National Bank, *Bankers Magazine*, 103 (July–Dec 1921) p 11
23. ACB, 'Fifty Years' Progress Toward an American Style in Architecture', *American Architect* 129 (Jan 5, 1926) p 49
24. ACB, 'American Architecture', *Op Cit* p 771
25. Banham, Reyner and others, *Buffalo Architecture: A Guide*, p 87
26. ACB, 'Twin Beacons of Amity', *Op Cit* p 179. A photograph showing Bossom before a model of the Liberty with a picture of the Tikal pyramid behind him is reproduced in *Building To The Skies*, p 17 and in Sharp, Dennis and Peter Wylde, 'Alfred Bossom and the American Skyscraper,' *Architectural Association Quarterly* 13 Nos 2/3 (1982) p 22
27. See for example ACB, *An Architectural Pilgrimage in Old Mexico*, ACB, 'Fifty Years' Progress Toward an American Style in Architecture'. *American Architect* 129 (Jan 5, 1926) p 4ff, and ACB, 'From Babel to Modern Skyscrapers', *Bankers Magazine* 110 (Jan-June 1925), pp 341–345
28. ACB, *Building To The Skies*, pp 18–19
29. ACB, 'Twin Towers of Amity', *Op Cit* p 178
30. ACB, 'Nicholas Roerich . . .', *Architectural Record* 50 No 2 (August 1921)
31. ACB, 'The Rebirth of Art and Architecture in Europe, A Review of the International Exposition at Paris', *The American Architect* 128 (August 28 1925) p 160ff
32. ACB, 'German Municipal Architecture, Illustrating the Work of Fritz Schumacher, Municipal Architect, Hamburg', *The American Architect* 132 (Dec 5, 1927) p 709ff 'Verticality in Design as Expressed in the Work of German Architects', *American Architect* 131 (Jan 20, 1927) pp 63–70
33. Bossom was an active figure in New York, teaching at the Master's Institute and serving as Treasurer (1924) and an Executive Committee member (1923) of the Architectural League and on various exhibit and catalogue committees from 1921 until 1926. He also established several awards and prizes awarded by the RIBA
34. Robinson, Cervin and Rosemarie Haag Bletter, *Skyscraper Style: Art Deco*, p 12 and footnote 23, p 31
35. ACB, *Building To The Skies*, p 9

Alfred C Bossom: Complete List of Buildings and Projects in the USA.

Connecticut

1915–17 Housing Development for the Remington Arms and Ammunition Company, Bridgeport

1917 Greenwich Trust Company, Greenwich

Undated Aaron House, Norwalk

Kansas

Undated Farmers National Bank, Salina

Louisiana

1920–21 Hibernia Bank and Trust Company, New Orleans. Associate architects: Favrot and Livaudais

Massachusetts

1921 House for Colonel Edward H R Green, Round Hill, South Dartmouth

New Jersey

c1912 Citizens National Bank, Long Branch

c1919 First National Bank, Bound Brook

1922 First National Bank of Jersey City, Jersey City

1924–25 Trenton Trust Company, Trenton

Undated Greenville Banking and Trust Company, Jersey City

Undated Liberty Trust Company, Newark

An early example of Alfred Bossom's workers' housing: 12 family apartment house, Bridgeport, Conn.

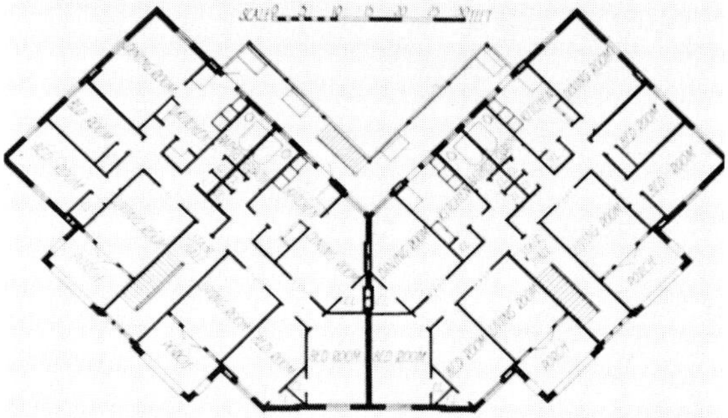

Typical Floor Plan

New York

1908–25 Restoration of Fort Ticonderoga, Lake Champlain

1910 House for Stephen H P Pell, Fort Ticonderoga

1911 Entrance Gateway and Stables for Colonel R M Thompson, Southampton, Long Island

1917 House for J W Harriman, Brookville, Long Island

1917–18 Housing for the United States Shipping Board, Port Jefferson, Long Island

c1918 Workers Housing for Bayles Shipyard, Port Jefferson, Long Island

1922 House for Henry D Whiton, Hewlett, Long Island

c1922 Huguenot Trust Company, New Rochelle

c1923 Yonkers Trust Company, Yonkers

1924 National Chautauqua County Bank, Jamestown

1924–25 Liberty Bank of Buffalo, Buffalo. Associate architects: Plummer and Mann

1925 Great Neck Trust Company, Great Neck, Long Island

1925–26 Hamilton National Bank, Queens Village, Long Island

Undated House for E L Young, Mill Kneck, Long Island

Undated Housing Development at Seneca Heights, Olean

House for S H P Pell at Fort Ticonderoga, c1910

Alfred C Bossom

Seneca Heights Housing

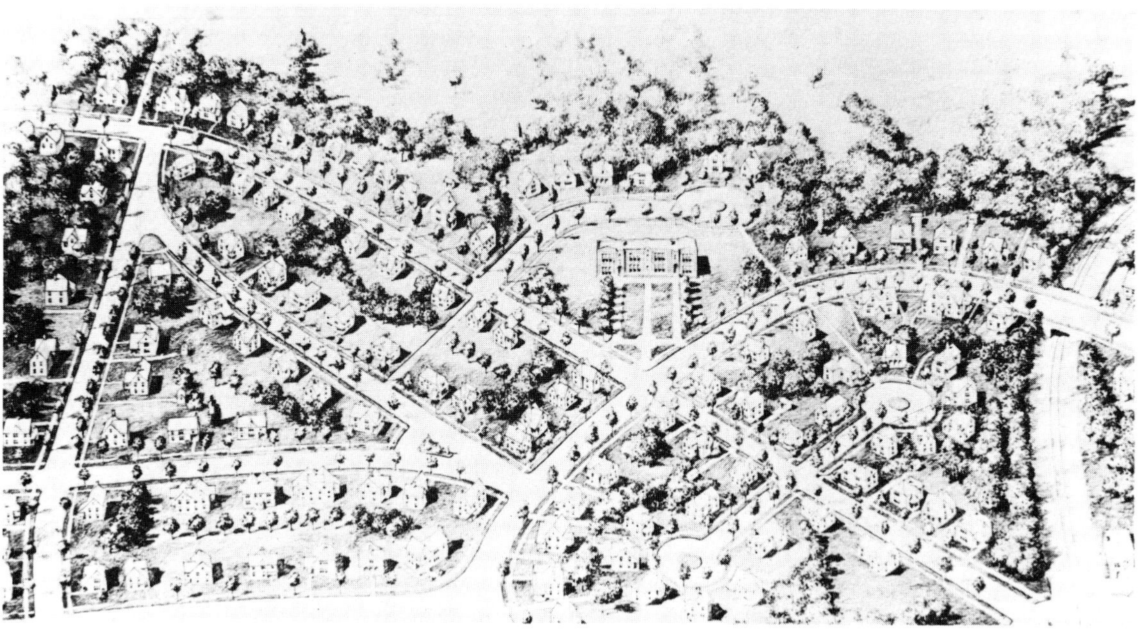

City of New York

c1919 Harlem Branch of Columbia Trust Company, Harlem

1919 Office Building for Gaston, Williams, and Wigmore, 35 Broadway

1919 Shop and Office Building for Jacob Doll and Sons, 110 West 42nd St

1919 Guaranty Trust Company's Bank of Asia, 35–39 Broadway

c1919 Interior decoration of Alfred C Bossom apartment, 21 East 82nd St

1920 Unbuilt project for a Memorial Bridge over the Hudson River

1920–21 Seaboard National Bank, corner of Broad and Beaver Streets. Now demolished.

1921 Apartment House at 168th St and Riverside Drive

1923 Apartment House at 150–54 East 49th St

c1924 Interior decoration of Alfred C Bossom apartment, 270 Park Avenue

Undated Columbia Knickerbocker Trust Company, Bronx

Jacob Doll & Sons Building, New York, 1919

Apartment House at 168th St, New York, 1921

North Carolina

1915	The Fidelity Bank, also known as the Geer Building, Durham. Now demolished
1915	The Merchants Bank, Durham
1922	Charlotte National Bank, Charlotte
1923	Wayne National Bank, Goldsboro

Ohio

Undated	Project for a House for S P Schloss

Pennsylvania

1904	Tenements for the United States Steel Company, Allegheny
c1905–06	Bowfront Buildings at 947 Pennsylvania Ave, Pittsburgh
1918	Colonial Trust Company, Philadelphia
1918	Titusville Trust Company, Titusville
1925	Farmers National Bank, Reading

Wayne National Bank at Goldsboro, N Carolina, 1923

United States National Bank at Galveston, Texas, 1924

Texas

1918	American Exchange National Bank, Dallas. Associate architects: Lang and Witchell
1922	Magnolia Petroleum Building, Dallas
1924	United States National Bank, Galveston
1924–25	Maple Terrace Apartments, Dallas. Associate architects: Thomson and Swaine
1924–26	'Adolphus III', alterations and extension to the Adolphus Hotel, Dallas. Associate architects: Thomson and Swaine
1925–26	The Petroleum Building, Houston. Associate architects: Briscoe, Dixon, and Sullivan
1926	Unbuilt project for the Goodhue Building, Beaumont
1927–28	San Jacinto Trust Company, Houston. Now demolished. Bossom acted as consultant to the architect Joseph W Northrop
Undated	Project for a House for A L Kramer, Dallas
Undated	Unbuilt project for an Auditorium, Dallas
Undated	Unbuilt project for a School of Diplomacy

TEXAS · BANK AND TRUST COMPANY
TEXAS BANK AND TRUST COMPANY

Project for an Auditorium at Dallas, Texas

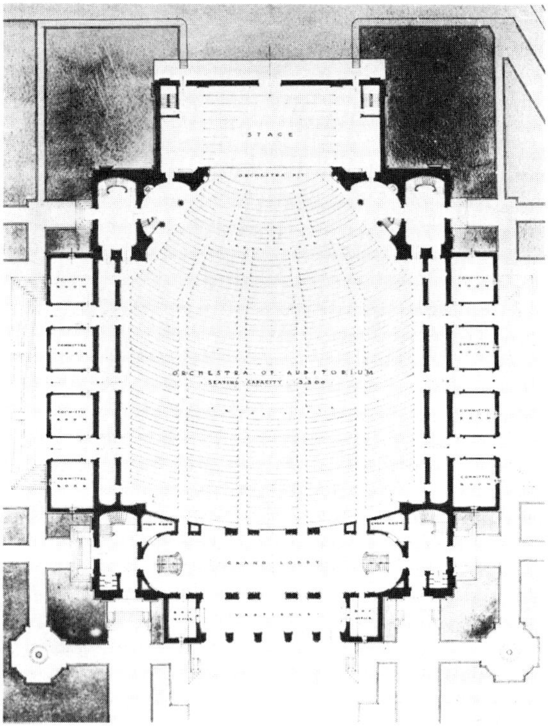

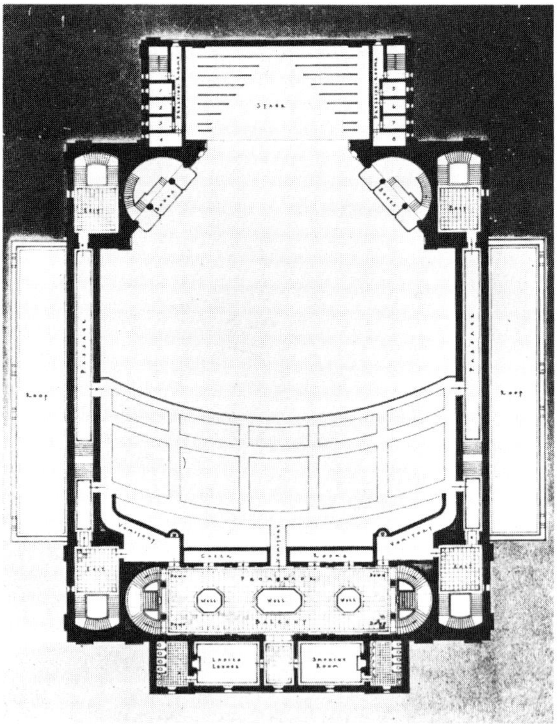

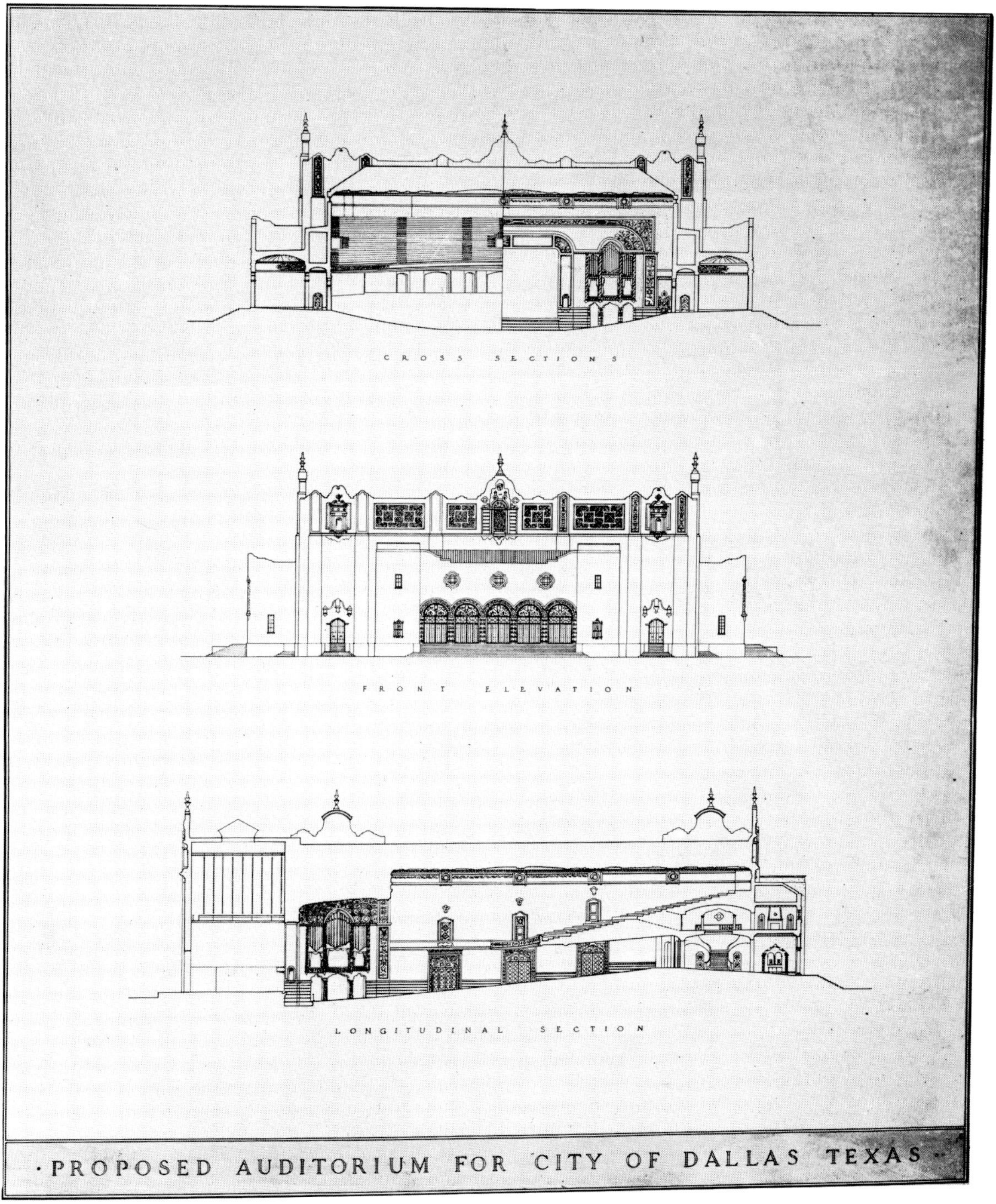

·PROPOSED AUDITORIUM FOR CITY OF DALLAS TEXAS·

Virginia

1912–13 First National Bank Building, Richmond. Also known as the Chesapeake and Ohio Railway Building. Associate architects: Clinton and Russell

1914 Alterations to the First National Bank, Lexington

c1915 Virginia Power and Railway Company Building, Richmond

1915–16 Lynchburg National Bank, Lynchburg

1916 The People's Bank, Harrisonburg

1918 Covington National Bank, Covington

1919 Citizens National Bank, Covington

1919–20 Virginia Trust Company, Richmond

1922 Monroe Terrace Apartments, Richmond

Undated Clifton Forge National Bank, Clifton Forge

Undated The Union Bank, Richmond. Now demolished

Washington DC

1924–25 Federal American National Bank. Associate architect: J H DeSibour

West Virginia

c1924 Kanawha Valley Bank and Trust Company, Charleston.

Monroe Terrace Apartments at Richmond, Virginia, 1922

Federal American National Bank at Washington DC, 1924–25

Biographical Notes on Alfred C Bossom

1881 Born, Islington, London, October 16. Educated, St Thomas Charterhouse School, London where he won gold medal and became head boy.

1897 Began studies at Regent Street Polytechnic, London.

1899 Takes job in London County Council (LCC) Architect's Office as draughtsman, later assistant architect. Attends Royal Academy Schools in evenings.

1903 Went to USA with George Crawley to work for H Phipps, on Carnegie Steel Mills, Pittsburgh. Intended to stay only a few months but in fact stayed until 1926.

1908 Began work on the Fort Ticonderoga restoration for the Pell family. One quarter of the Fort was completed in time for the international Tercentenary celebrations, 1909.

1910 Married Emily, daughter of Samuel Bayne, President of National Seaboard Bank, New York. Around the same time and before World War I he designed several bank buildings in Virginia.

1911 Birth of son, Bruce.

1914 Bossom volunteered to enlist at outbreak of war but was told to stay in US and use his contacts to promote good relations. During war was involved in Remington Arms and Ammunition Co, Bridgeport, Conn, in building homes for 50,000 workers.

1918 Resumed architectural practice in New York with offices at 680 Fifth Avenue. Specialisation in bank buildings led to a flood of commissions in various parts of the US.
Apartment at 21 East 82nd St, New York City.
Constantly visited Europe.
Birth of son, Clive.

1919 Elected member, Architectural League of New York.

1921– Visit to Mexico; recorded in sketchbooks.

1922 Birth of son, Doric.

1924 Fellowship: Royal Institute of British Architects. Trip down Yukon River through British Columbia begins interest in collecting Indian objects. Visit to Basque area of Spain; recorded in sketchbooks. Treasurer: Architectural League of New York. Publication of *An Architectural Pilgrimage in Old Mexico*.
Apartment at 270 Park Avenue, New York City.

1925 Visited World Exposition in Paris.

1926 Returned to England in Autumn, 1926. He never again practised architecture but soon commenced a political career.

1927 Adopted as Conservative candidate for Hackney. Co-opted onto Housing Committee of LCC.

1929 Lost parliamentary election at Hackney. Became Alderman of LCC, 1930–34 and Chairman of Slum Clearance Sub-Committee.

1931 Elected Conservative member for Maidstone, Kent.

1932 Lost wife and eldest son Bruce in plane crash.

1934 Publication of *Building to the Skies: The Romance of the Skyscraper*, Studio, London and New York.

1939 During World War II served as one of 28 members of the National Expenditure Committee to oversee efficiency of spending, 1939–45.

1943 Went to USA as leader of fact finding mission for 'Portal' Mission to see prefabricated and machine made housing etc. Flew some 33,000 miles during six weeks, in coast-to-coast survey. Report published (see Bibliography) in 1944.

1948 Publication of *Our House: An Introduction to Parliamentary Procedure*, PUP, London.

1952 Hon LL.D, Pittsburgh University.

1953 Created a Baronet during Coronation Year.

1957 Chairman, Royal Society of Arts, 1957–59.

1959 Retired from Parliament at 1959 election having represented Maidstone for 28 years.

1960 Created Life Peer, taking title 'Lord Bossom of Maidstone'.

1964 Vice-President, Royal Society of Arts.

1965 Died at home in London on September 4, aged 83.

Select Bibliography

Books by Alfred C Bossom

Building to the Skies: the Romance of the Skyscraper, London and New York: The Studio Ltd, 1934

An Architectural Pilgrimage in old Mexico, New York: Charles Scribner's, 1924

Our House: An Introduction to Parliamentary Procedure, London: People's University Press, 1948

Bossom Family Christmas Cards 1915–1947, Privately printed in London, 1948

A Bird's Eye view of Europe in 1937, Maidstone, *Kent Messenger*, 1937

Some Reminiscences: Alfred Bossom, Maidstone, Kent. Reprinted from the *Kent Messenger*, June–August, 1959

Report (largely compiled by Alfred Bossom)
'Methods of Building in the USA' The Report of a mission appointed by the Minister of Works, (Portal Mission), London: HMSO, 1944

Magazine articles

'The Requirements of a Modern Bank Building', *Bankers Magazine*, Vol 83, No 11, Nov 1911, pp 658–662

'The Housing of Employees', *Architectural Forum*, Aug 1917

Boyd, J T, 'The Country House of J W Harriman Esq, Brookville, Long Island: Alfred C Bossom, Architect', *Architectural Record*, Vol 43, No 1, Jan 1918, pp 2–21

'Homes for Wartime Workers', *Architectural Record*, Vol 44, Sept 1918, pp 214–224

'The Office Building of Gaston, Williams & Wigmore, Inc, on Lower Broadway, New York City', *Architectural Record*, Vol 45, Apr 1919, pp 356–365

'The Bank Doorway', *Bankers Magazine*, No 99, Jul–Dec 1919, pp 73ff

'Apartment of Alfred C Bossom, Architect', *Architectural Record*, Vol 46, Aug 1919, pp 171–173

'Portfolio of Current Architecture: Jacob Doll & Sons Building, New York + Titusville Trust Company's Building, Titusville, Pa', *Architectural Record*, Vol 47, June 1920, pp 544–549

Imlay, R, 'The Proposed Victory Bridge over the Hudson between New York City and Weekawken: A C Bossom, Architect', *Architectural Record*, Vol 48, Sept 1920, pp 219–223

'Proposed Memorial Bridge Across the Hudson River at New York', *American Architect*, Vol 119–2, No 2363, Apr 6, 1921, pp 423–425

'In the Garden of S H P Pell, Fort Ticonderoga, New York', *American Architect*, Vol 119–2, No 2365, Apr 20, 1921, p 479

'New Home of the Seaboard National Bank', *Bankers Magazine*, No 103, Jul–Dec 1921, pp 113ff

'Virginia Trust Company's New Home', *Bankers Magazine*, No 103, Jul–Dec 1921, pp 561–568

'Home of S H P Pell, Esq, Fort Ticonderoga, New York', *American Architect*, Vol 120, No 2371, Jul 6, 1921, 2 plates

'Nicholas K Roerich: His Art in its Bearing on Mural Decoration in America', *Architectural Record*, Vol 50, No 2, Aug 1921, pp 83–92

'Virginia & Tate Trust Co Building, Richmond, Va', *Architectural Forum*, Vol 35, No 2, Aug 1921, 4 photos

Price, M, 'The Seaboard National Bank, New York, NY', *Architectural Record*, Vol 51, May 1922, pp 476–485

'Portfolio of Modern Bank Work', Supplements to the *Bankers Magazine.* No 105, Jul–Dec 1922; No 106, Jan–Jun 1923; No 107, Jan–Jun 1923; No 109, Jul–Dec 1924; No 111, Jul–Dec 1925

'House of Col E H R Green, South Dartmouth, Mass', *American Architect*, Vol 122, No 2398, Jul 19, 1922, 1 plate

'First National Bank, Jersey City, NJ', *Architectural Record*, Vol 52, Aug 1922, pp 104–107

'The System of an American Architect's Office', *Architects' Journal*, Vol 56, Oct 4, 1922, pp 442–445

'First National Bank Building, Richmond, Va', *The Builder*, Vol 123, Nov 17, 1922, pp 734–735 and 739

'Three American Business Buildings designed by Alfred C Bossom', *Architectural Review*, Vol 52, Dec 1922, pp 150–154 (Contents: 1. The First National Bank of Jersey City 2. The Seaboard National Bank of New York 3. The Magnolia Petroleum Company Building, Dallas, Texas)

'Wayne National Bank, Goldsboro, North Carolina', *Bankers Magazine*, No 106, Jan–Jul 1923, pp 736–738

'Buildings for the Colonial Trust Co, Philadelphia, Pa', *American Architect*, Vol 115–2, No 2270, Jun 23, 1919, pp 877–878

'Three Banks by Alfred C Bossom, Architect', *Architectural Record*, Vol 55, Mar 1924, pp 263–267

'Decoration: An Apartment at 21E, 82nd Street, New York', *Architectural Review*, Vol 56, Dec 1924, pp 231–233

'Apartment House, 108 Street and Riverside Drive, New York', *American Architect*, Vol 123, No 2418, Apr 25, 1923, 4 plates

'New Senior Officers Quarters of the Seaboard', *Bankers Magazine*, No 108, Jan–Jun 1924, pp 1013–16

'America's National Architecture', *American Architect*, Vol 128, Jul 29, 1925, pp 77–83 (Reprinted in *The Architect*, Aug 21, 1925)

'From Babel to Modern Skyscrapers', *Bankers Magazine*, No 110, Jan–Jun 1925, pp 341–345

'The Rebirth of Art and Architecture in Europe: A review of the International Exhibition at Paris (1925)', *American Architect*, Vol 128, No 2479, Aug 26, 1925, pp 161–166

'New Home of the Liberty Bank in Buffalo', *Bankers Magazine*, No 111, Jul–Dec 1925, pp 994ff

'Trenton Trust Company, Trenton, NJ', *Architecture*, Vol 52, Dec 1925, pp 177–181

'Fifty Years' Progress Toward an American Style in Architecture', *American Architect*, Vol 129, No 2488, Jan 5, 1926, pp 43–49

'Twin Beacons of Amity as Reflected in the Architectural Design of the Liberty Bank of Buffalo', *American Architect*, Vol 129, No 2489, Jan 20, 1926, pp 177–182

'Restoration of the Ancient City of Tikal Guatemala', *American Architect*, Vol 129, No 2491, Feb 20, 1926, p 266

'Verticality in Design as Expressed in the Work of German Architects', *American Architect*, Vol 131, No 2513, Jan 20, 1927, pp 63–70

'American Architecture', *Journal of the Royal Society of Arts*, Jun 8, 1928, pp 761–784

'San Jacinto Trust Building, Houston, Texas', *American Architect*, Vol 134, No 5, 1928, pp 283–290

Thompson, W H, 'Exhibition of American Skyscrapers'. (Review of exhibition of photographs loaned by Alfred C Bossom at the RIBA, 22 July–2 August, 1929), *RIBA Journal*, Vol 36, No 7, Aug 1929, pp 730–732

Catalogue, *Exhibition of Arts and Crafts of British Columbia Indians* (Lent by Mr & Mrs A C Bossom), Imperial Institute, March 27 to May 20, 1929. This article was expanded and reprinted in a mimeographed catalogue for a further Exhibition at the Imperial Institute in 1954

'The Architects' Registration Bill "Talked Out" in the House of Commons', (report of the speech of A C Bossom), *Architect & Building News*, Vol 150, Apr 16, 1937, pp 81–83

'Can Buildings Cost Less?', *National Builder*, Jul 1927, pp 288–290

'Colonial Williamsburg: How Americans Handle a Restoration', *Architect & Building News*, Vol 169, Mar 27, 1942, pp 229–230 and in *The Builder*, Vol 162, Mar 27, 1942, pp 273–275

'Progress in Architecture', *The Studio*, No 125, April/May, 1943, pp 139–143

'Post-war Building', *Design for Britain* Series – 2nd Series, 1944, Vol 2:27 – whole issue, London/ Letchworth: Dent, 1944

Obituaries: *The Times*, Sept 6, 1965
The Builder, Sept 10, 1965, p 545

Sharp, D, & P Wylde, 'Alfred Bossom and the American Skyscraper', *AA Quarterly*, Vol 13, No 2/3, 1982, pp 22–32

Alfred C Bossom: Other references

Burchard, John and Bush-Brown, Albert, *The Architecture of America*, Boston and Toronto: Little Brown & Co, 1961, pp 351–352

Robinson, Cervin and Rosemarie Haag Bletter, *Skyscraper Style: Art Deco, New York*, Oxford University Press, 1975

Mathis, David and Susan Grayson, *Celebrating an Enduring Past: An Architectural Walking Tour in Richmond, Virginia.* Virginia Commonwealth University, 1978

Banham, Reyner and others, *Buffalo Architecture: A Guide*, Cambridge Mass and London: MIT Press, 1981

Chambers, S Allen Jr, *Lynchburg, An Architectural History*, Charlottesville, Virginia: University Press of Virginia, 1981

Winthrop, Robert P, *Architecture in Downtown Richmond*, Historic Richmond Foundation, 1982

Sources and Documents

Those Early Years

Although Alfred Bossom was a prolific writer and produced in his lifetime articles on subjects ranging from primitive art, building efficiency methods to straightforward political speeches, it was not until the period towards the end of his life that he recorded his early years in any detail. The Kentish Gazette, *the local newspaper serving his own constituency at Maidstone, Kent, ran a series of articles on his life's work and ambitions in 1963. These articles however did not dwell at any length on his early training as an architect and business man. However, it seems that these published reminiscences provoked in him a desire to put the record straight on his 'early years'. Around the time of the publication of the* Kentish Gazette *articles he began to draft chapters for his autobiography. These helped to fill in the details of his background and education as well as his inventiveness and creative energy prior to the commencement of his highly successful professional career. The following extract brings his story up to his departure from England to the United States. It was never published before and is included here in an edited form.*

Looking back over more than eighty years, it seems that my life has been divided into four clearly discernible phases.

First school days and early architectural training until the time I went to America. Next the twenty-three years during which I practised architecture in the United States. Then my return home to England and election to the House of Commons where for the next twenty-eight years I remained as the Member for Maidstone, Kent, and finally the varied activities and interests since I left the Commons.

On a Sunday morning in October 1881 I was born a not very robust infant and during the first years suffered attacks of bronchitis and asthma. Had it not been for the self-sacrificing care of my dear Mother, this story would not have been written. . . .

In due time I was sent to a prep school, the Home and Colonial, which in those days specialised in taking as pupils the children of Britishers who had gone out to look after matters in the Colonies and Dominions. Of course here a spirit of loyalty to the Empire was strongly encouraged, so much so that I have never lost awareness of the vital importance of closest friendship with the Empire (as it then was), and the Commonwealth of today. My habitual place just then seemed to be bottom of the class but after a time and with the unfailing parental help I started to do better. . . .

After prep school I was sent to St Thomas, Charterhouse (which no longer exists) and started my serious education. At that date long school holidays were not the rule and slowly I began to intensify my studies until I at last achieved a better place in class, and incidentally at the end of my time there had a surprising experience. Absolutely no use at sport (I clearly remember the time the top eleven from an educational point of view played the cricket top eleven and although the former were sadly beaten I managed to get the biggest score I ever made – three runs!) I got on with my studies and won the Gold Medal as head boy. . . .

At Charterhouse more scientific subjects were covered than was usual in those long ago years and I suppose coming from a family in which, more particularly on my father's side, there seems to have been a sense of the adventurous, I felt peculiarly at home with such training. A cousin of my Father's had been one of the small group of cavalrymen, the first white men to ride through the Khyber Pass; another relation took part in one of the early yacht races around West Africa and had the gruesome experience of arriving there as cannibals were devouring the crew of the yacht that had managed to get ahead of his. . . .

Of course I was prone to the normal schoolboy's interests and at one period became very enthusiastic about collecting Laclance cells. I managed to get enough of these for my bedroom to be lighted by electricity and, strange as it may seem today, this caused a lot of excitement and was a quite unique thing for a boy to have then.

A student project design for an entrance gateway project for a collegiate building.

One day a friend of mine, Emanuel Percy Hussey (a most ingenious youth with a Father interested in the development of barometers and thermometers), and I decided there should be airships; no doubt we had been influenced by Leonardo da Vinci! Between us we set to work and made a tin tube about 18″ long by 6″ wide with pointed ends; this we fitted with a top in which we stuck about six vertical masts each with a small propellor. In the bottom of the tube we put a stick encircled with rubber bands which connected the masts. The action of winding up the stick and pulling it out revolved the small masts and the tin tube rose in the air and floated around for ten or twenty seconds. We of course fondly hoped this was perhaps the first airship made by boys.

Physiology, mechanics, the laws of health and astronomy, all had their turn of strong appeal, but my real love was art, particularly drawing which I doubtless inherited from my Father who would illustrate his ideas quite successfully. I can remember at a quite early age drawing comic strips for funny papers such as 'Ally Sloper' and 'Comic Cuts' and in time such efforts brought me in a tidy income for a youngster. Automatically, I followed these with caricatures of prominent political characters.

I was careful with my pennies and worked like a dog to try to win boys' competitions which often gave money prizes. When about eleven years old I won my first LCC Scholarship which paid my education fees at that time, and left some for my own allowance. About eighteen months later I got an extension of this and in a further year was lucky enough to be one of the youngest pupils to win what was then called an 'intermediate scholarship' and could then have chosen to go to almost any school.

Now lest all of this makes the reader think I had an abnormally good brain, let me enlighten him and say at once that I was born with a freakish memory. It was soon found that after reading a page of any book about three times I could pretty well repeat it word for word. Needless to say, this played a tremendously helpful part in the things I tried to do and I only wish I had it now! . . .

At the tender age of sixteen my youthful ambition was to become a doctor and, without consulting anyone, I made enquiries of several medical schools and hospitals. Naturally enough, nothing came of this unorthodox approach and I have never forgotten the day I was rejected by London University Hospital and went home to bed depressed and worried; though before morning came, thinking of my ability to draw I had determined to be an architect. Again my impatience had to be curbed, this time by the Head Master (Banister Fletcher) of King's College, Strand, the leading architectural school in London. He was very kind to me at the interview but equally most emphatic in his guidance. 'Better go back to school and get more general education before attempting to specialise in a profession' he advised.

But the seed was sown and I was anxious to get ahead and so I thanked him for his advice and began searching around for a place where I could put my ideas to the test. Eventually, I discovered the Regent Street Polytechnic (founded by the grandfather of the present Quintin Hogg) which had just started a small architectural studio for about a dozen or so young enthusiasts like myself who could work as hard as they liked. Mr Charles Mitchell the Head, after 'vetting' me let me join them, and looking back it was one of the happiest periods of my life studying all day long and attending evening classes; in fact from the age of 16 to 21 I did not join in any social activities. My father allowed me one room in the house given up entirely to a great drawing board where, after evening classes, I could draw and make my architectural studies until 4 in the morning when I would go to bed, getting up again at 8 am. For five years I did this except on Saturdays when I worked until midnight and then went to bed and stayed there until early Monday morning when the week's routine started again. This may have been bad for my health but it enabled me to do about half as much work again as the average student and in consequence win quite a few medals for various subjects.

Among the few who received their groundwork in the little architectural studio in Regent

DESIGN·FOR
THE·ENTRANCE
GATEWAY·TO·A
COLLEGIATE
BUILDING
ALFRED·G·BISSOM

Street was Albert Richardson (the late Professor Sir Albert Richardson) who was to become an eminent architect and well-known President of the Royal Academy. We became good friends – a privilege which I was able to enjoy throughout his lifetime. Richardson was never a student in the Academy Schools but went out teaching and was a most charming man and a brilliant raconteur; in fact in latter years he became almost better known for his stories than for his architecture! Another of the pupils was Vincent Harris, later Treasurer of the Royal Academy.

As I think back over the years it seems to me that the Regent Street Polytechnic was one of the most successful architectural study schools it could have been my fortune to attend. My drawing ability was invaluable and as well as working on the drawing board I studied the trades employed in the construction of a building – brick-laying, carpentry, plumbing, modelling and so forth. Possibly through so much concentrated effort, a day came when my name was carved on a marble doorpost inside the Polytechnic as their first distinguished architectural pupil and I was enabled to take the students' entrance examination for the Architectural School of the Royal Academy of Arts. In this I was extremely fortunate for I managed to pass, I was told, at a earlier age than had been done before. . . .

In about 1899 the Polytechnic was notified of openings for draughtsmen in the Housing Department of the LCC. Mr Mitchell told me to try for one of these jobs which I did with success, and started to earn the handsome salary of 15/– a week, working there during the daytime and studying each evening at the RA. This incidentally was the only employed job I ever held. My first work there was to lay out the drainage and plumbing for the Battersea Bridge buildings, where I am led to believe it still works! Another task was when the Council picked a certain Matthew Dawson and I to design a Technical School. We took a great chance I am afraid, and designed the floor construction as a series of shallow concrete domes (one of the earliest times this was done), but it worked. . . .

During this period I was following, with some fellow students, a procedure known then as 'taking in washing'. In those days architects would sometimes decide to compete for a proposed building and would get students to work on designs for them. Some of us were fortunate in this and won competitions for quite big buildings; not of course for ourselves, but the buildings were built to our design from working drawings made in the architect's office. A personal prize I was successful in winning was given by the British Institution and was worth £200; for this, I had only two weeks to get the draw-

An item in an art nouveau style from an early scrap book compiled by Alfred Bossom, c 1898.

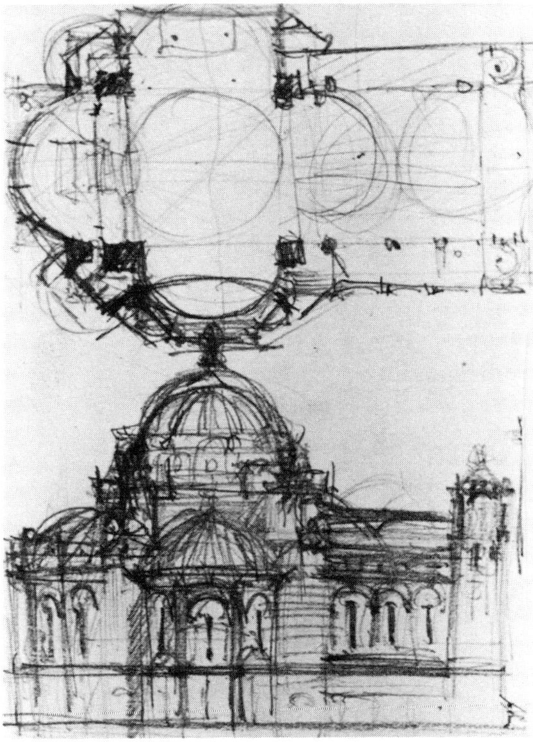

One of the earliest drawings made by Alfred Bossom is for a church project, perhaps a design subject at the Royal Academy Schools?

A student design project for a 'Royal Philosophical Society'.

ings done and had to work night and day.

All we young architects were fascinated by the competitions then being held, which included such buildings as the South Kensington Museum, the refacing of Buckingham Palace and development of the Mall etc, and we were impressed by the possibilities ahead which we ourselves hoped to realise some day. . . .

Another interesting job was being able to put into use my Academy training in perspective drawing for artists who needed architectural background scenes drawn in charcoal on canvas before painting in the colour and figures.

This hotpotch of activities led me to an unusual result. The great American ironmaster, Andrew Carnegie, went from the USA to Germany in 1898 and there found a scientist who could analyse steel, a most abstruse and exceptional activity. He hired the man and took him back to Pittsburgh where his partner, Henry Phipps, objected and said they could not afford this profession. But Carnegie insisted and his decision led to their firm growing in a few years into the largest steel works in existence – the great United States Steel Company.

In 1902 Henry Phipps (who often related this story to me) informed Carnegie that he could do no more for the steel works as they were the biggest of their kind in the world. But he determined to do something for the workers who were living in very unsatisfactory homes at that time. He asked a friend of his, George Abraham Crawley, a brilliant man, to take him round London, including a visit to the Royal Academy School. There he asked the headmaster, Phene Spiers, if they had anyone capable of preparing a layout for the rehousing of workers of the steel Company so that they could be literally picked up out of Pittsburgh and moved to the nearby town of Alleghenny. Spiers listened and said 'Yes, we have a student who can do that' and I was the one!

Thus in 1903, at the age of 22, I was taken by George Crawley to America, and using the knowledge I had gained from our LCC, laid out the housing arrangements for thousands of steel workers.

Before that time, my family had always intended that I should go to South Africa where my Mother's cousin, Sir Siddons Graves, held a quite prominent architectural position and was connected with the Concentration Camps required due to the Boer War. But unfortunately, he had great trouble and came back to England where he soon afterwards died. This caused sadness and disappointment and so my unexpected call to America fitted in to the general scheme of my life, which was to work abroad.

They were good, those early years.

A sketch turned into a Christmas card.

A page from a sketch book showing the Tower of the Rosaire, Bruges, c 1898.

A page from one of Bossom's early sketch books, c 1898.

5-storey tenement houses designed by Alfred Bossom for Henry Phipps of Allegany, Pa.

The Housing of Employees

Having emigrated to the United States in order to build workers' housing for the Carnegie Steel Works in Pennsylvania, Bossom continued to specialise in this kind of project throughout the early part of his career. During the First World War the unprecedented boom in war-related industries brought him major commissions: among other schemes Bossom built virtually complete small towns for shipyard workers in New York State and for the Remington Arms and Ammunition Co in Connecticut. This long and detailed article, of which we have included edited extracts, was written in 1917 and brings together his accumulated experience in building these schemes. It is clear that he was involved not only in their architectural design but in the whole process of conception, land acquisition and funding.

As early as 1695 John Bellers, a prominent Quaker, published a pamphlet in London entitled, "Proposals and Husbandry, with Profit for the Rich and Plentiful Living for the Poor, and a Good Education for Youth, which will be an Advantage to the Government by the Increase of the People and their Riches." This old idea has long since passed the experimental stage and is now recognized as an economic, for it is the domestic life and not the factory life that gives the character to a country.

It is a fact that in the same ratio as the power of the great nations of the past developed, so the homes of the poor became more and more unsatisfactory. In the great Reformation movement the houses of the rich took on vast improvements, but the dwellings of the workers became more unhygienic than the huts of the primitive uncivilized tribes.

Considerable agitation and a number of laws were passed in England in the latter half of the last century; but when a royal commission sat to investigate conditions, it was proven that laws alone would not help the habitations of workers, and this

Housing for workers at Bayles Shipyard, Port Jefferson, Long Island, 1918.

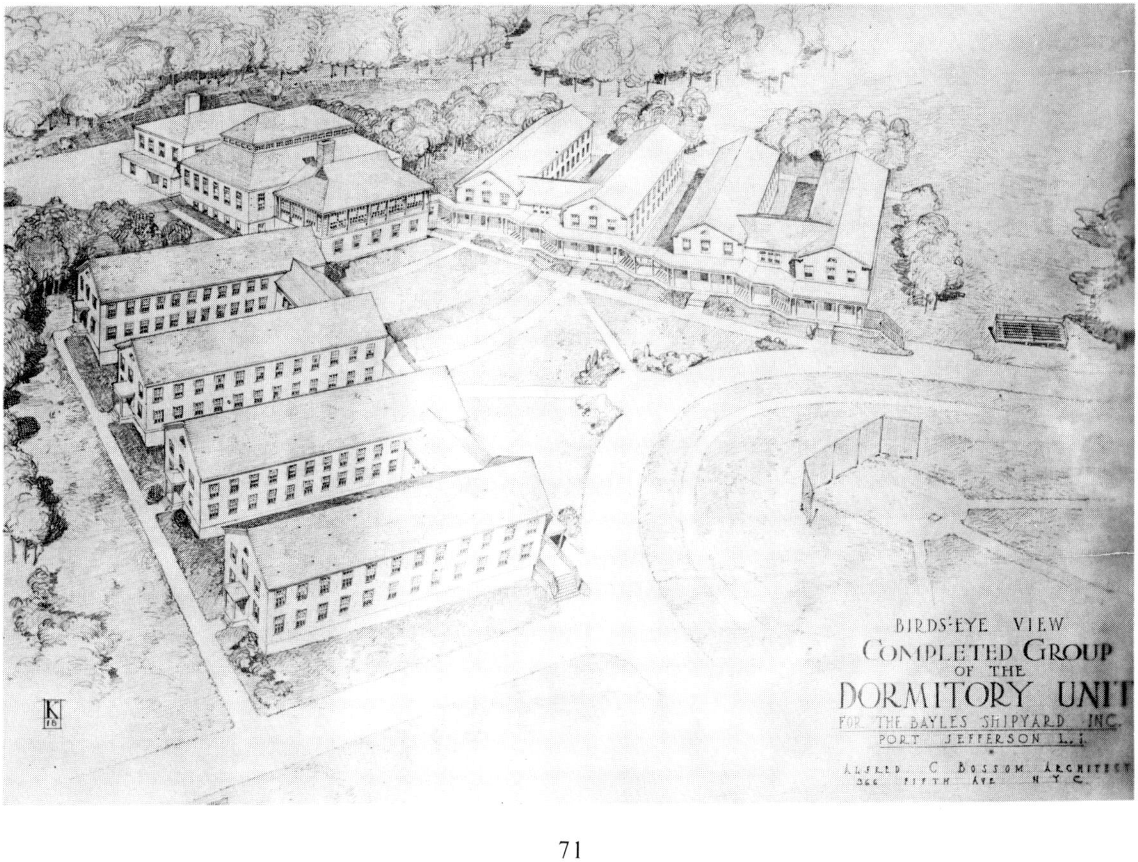

same condition prevails today. It is the duty of those responsible for the well being of employees to make every effort to raise the standard of living to a level commensurate with the power and wealth of the nation.

Those great purifiers, light and air, which are provided in unlimited quantities, will do untold work unless the perverse ingenuity of man imposes some almost insurmountable obstacle. It is possible for all humans to benefit from ample light and air in their places of work, rest, or play if they are only taught their value.

Profit sharing also has gone beyond the experimental stage and in some form or another is in active operation in many of the large labour employing concerns. Where this sharing takes the form of giving the employee the opportunity of securing a suitable home in a desirable location at a reasonable price, it immediately reacts to the benefit of the employer in promoting greater efficiency among those employed.

In addition to the home with its light and air, two great wants in the lives of wage earners are space and beauty, and these give such tremendous returns in relation to their cost that it is hard to comprehend why they so seldom exist.

In fairness it must be said that all employees do not live under conditions that are unsatisfactory, but as the great majority of large manufacturing centers have grown up around factories at the instance of the speculator, and without regard to important economic requirements, the percentage whose living conditions are good is exceedingly small. Even in the few instances where ideal conditions may be said to exist, it can readily be shown that at least one family in ten is overcrowded. No manufacturer who is endeavoring to produce the best possible results would consider allowing the operatives to work in badly lighted, unsanitary, or avoidable unsatisfactory conditions, irrespective of compulsory legal requirements to do otherwise. The average working day is eight hours and during the remaining sixteen the worker is often compelled by circumstances that could easily be remedied to live under conditions that tend to place his working efficiency at the lowest possible level. Newcomers in any section if they are going to be assimilated must be brought up to the desired standard during the sixteen hours outside the shop. A new operative obtaining employment in a new location is compelled to take any accommodation available, and if this is bad he will remove quickly, causing loss to himself and to the employer, or correspondingly lower the standard.

Remington Housing Development at Bridgeport, Connecticut, 1915–17

A man not getting refreshing sleep, worrying about his home affairs, or compelled to pass the greater portion of his time amid long monotonous rows of dreary shacks – without a blade of grass or a green tree, and often where even paint is a thing of long ago – cannot be expected to have initiative or be able to produce the same result as a man not so handicapped, aside from the injurious mental, moral, and health effects.

Utopia is not to be found nor is the millennium to be suddenly produced; but it is within the power of almost all large employers of labor, and with benefit to themselves, to look into the way

Plans of typical workers' houses.

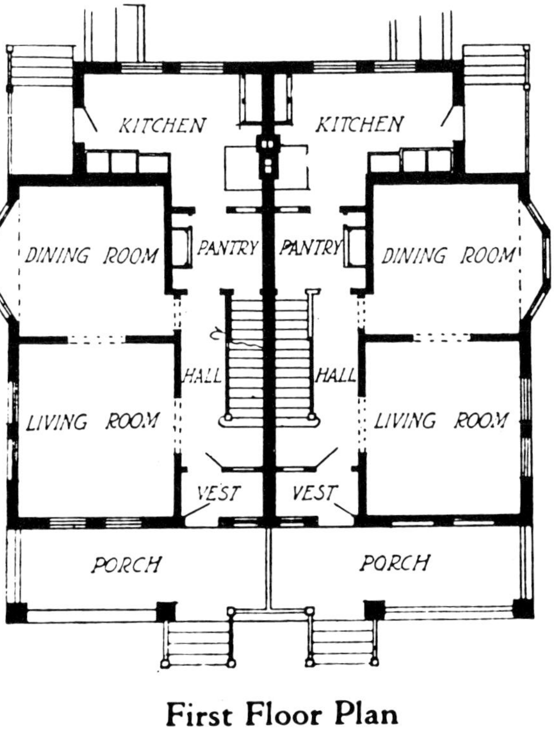

First Floor Plan

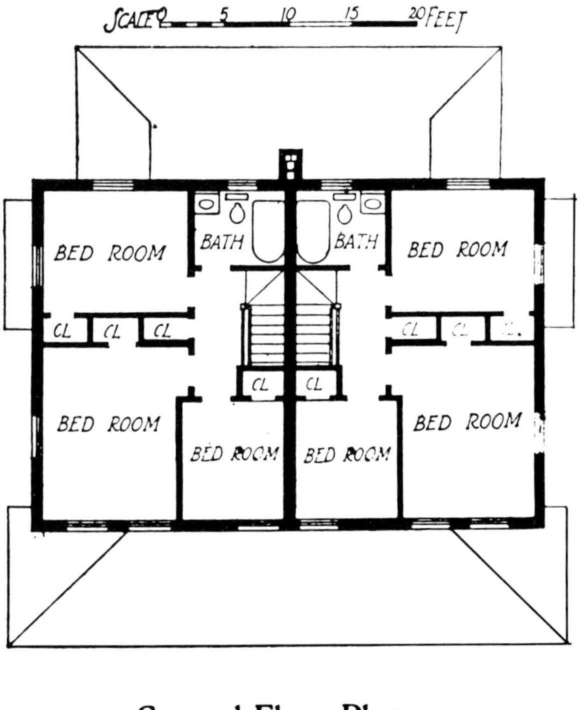

Second Floor Plan

their people are living the two-thirds of their lives spent outside the workshop. We conserve our coal and forests, in fact all natural resources, and yet hardly any effort is made to conserve the health and mentality of the great majority of the human population.

Better conditions have been promoted in office, loft, and factory buildings than in small residences, for in the former the profit earned from the workers makes it possible for the speculator to receive a larger return in rent; but in domestic buildings the alcove room without a window is still a favorite with the speculator, and that fire-trap, the "three-decker" tenement house, has outlived its former contemporary, the wooden workroom, by many years.

While the employee is directly under the observation of the employer, he is looked after as carefully as a machine is studied to produce the most satisfactory output. Experience and constructive thought are now teaching that this human being must be also studied and aided during that part of the day when he is not occupied by his work. Satisfactory homes amid desirable surroundings, if unobtainable otherwise, can be provided advantageously by the employer. When this is accomplished, every inducement should be undertaken to make the occupants take pride in their community and get the most benefit from the investment made on their behalf.

Co-operation of this type leads to a more satisfactory understanding between employer and employee, which makes strikes or lockouts less likely and creates a state of mutual interest. The employer is comparatively assured of a permanent, dependable nucleus of labor in rush times, and the employee is correspondingly assured of a uniform low rent for the best accommodation it is possible to obtain. . . .

The actual housing of employees may be accomplished by several methods, such as the use of some old property through renovation and modeling; by individual one and two family houses; by the one family house in rows, not detached; three-story houses with one family over the other, accommodating as many families as the size of the house and the number of units joined together permit, and the latest type of tenement house. These with their various modifications and special buildings – such as the men's barrack hotels, the children's crèches, dormitories, and recreation homes – cover the possibilities.

The type of house suitable for the West Virginia coal miner differs entirely from the house needed by the highly paid mechanic in a manufacturing town of Ohio; but the underlying fundamentals remain unchanged, and with knowledge of the operatives, their scale of wages, hours of labor, and location of the plant and available land, it is not difficult to decide upon the most desirable type of housing to provide. . . .

Under ideal circumstances the compact, conveniently arranged, individual house for one family, in its own small plot of ground, with air and light on all sides, is the best type, and in congested districts the best varies from this down to the three-story tenement house, which gives the cheapest rent where land has much value.

The division of the land naturally varies with the several forms of improvement; for instance, on a property divided into lots 50 by 100 feet, and improved with three-story buildings, not more than between six and seven such units per acre are possible. Thus in this type of improvement a maximum of twenty families to the acre is all that can be considered. In the case of the individual, isolated houses which have garden or playground space, eight to twelve per acre can be installed; but if the land is reasonably cheap, as few as four per acre is a more desirable number.

The two family isolated house has the advantage of giving the tenant owner the opportunity of getting an income from the one-half while living in the other, and the addition of one or two rooms for lodgers often makes a house more desirable in spite of being more expensive to the original renter. Single houses in rows are satisfactory, provided the rows are not too long – six to eight houses form the best group. This type has the disadvantage of having no side ground, but is easier to heat, and having party walls, which should run up through the roof, requires only simple roof arrangements. The individual house is capable of being rented or sold to employees at a comparatively low price. . . .

The monetary value of available land has to be judged in conjunction with the cost per unit of the most desirable form of building; thus three-story buildings in very cheap semi-country property would be preordained to failure, although it would show up very well on paper, and yet under proper conditions of development the same land could be used with immediate and marked success.

In London and Liverpool, and in congested cities like New York and Pittsburgh, five-story tenement "walk-up" buildings have been built with success, but this type of improvement should be undertaken now only after most mature consideration, as the American workman is daily learning to avoid inconvenience, and a strictly American community would most likely refuse to occupy the accommodation provided above the third floor except at a very low rental.

To determine the most desirable form the improvement can take in addition to all the previously enumerated considerations, the value of the available land must be considered; similarly the size of families, for although the average be five persons, with certain nationalities this varies, and the proportion of unmarried varies in different localities. For instance, men without families are always more numerous in new undertakings and these have to be cared for either by the married men or in special barrack hotels built for the purpose.

The usual proportion of unattached men to married is as one to two, but all figures should be carefully checked in the actual locality, for this bears a decided relation to the wages earned by the different grades of men and therefore to the rent that they can afford to pay for their homes.

One-third of the wages is found to be the ultimate maximum that workmen can possibly pay for purchasing the home, taxes, and insurance, and not above 25 per cent for renting. . . .

A safe return and a conservative investment must be looked for, not a real estate speculation producing abnormal profits. A sinking fund must be created, if the accommodation provided is only rented, to reduce it to its actual real estate value in a number of years, and a fund to cover contingencies if the same be sold. If rented only, long term leases should not be made, or employees leaving the company could still occupy their houses to the detriment of those actually engaged. A reduction system which by periods allows bonuses to apply toward the reduction of the mortgage, provided the employee has continuous employment, and the re-purchasing power of the owners on a certain understood basis should the employee leave the employer, are features that are well to introduce into the financial scheme.

By these and similar methods the employee constantly receives advantages for good and continued services, and the owner benefits in having employees better equipped physically and mentally.

From: 'The Housing of Employees', *Architectural Forum*, Aug 1917.

The Requirements of a Modern Bank Building

As well as contributing to professional architectural magazines Alfred Bossom prepared special articles for technical and commercial publications. Understandably, being a specialist in bank buildings and having married a banker's daughter, one of his primary concerns was with the designing and building of banks in various parts of America. His article 'The Requirements of a Modern Bank Building' offered advice for those seeking new buildings to house existing institutions and gave advice on the re-construction of old buildings to meet the requirements of a modern bank.

At this time Bossom was designing his first large bank buildings such as the First National Bank of Richmond, Virginia, constructed in 1912–13.

Having been requested to describe for the readers of the BANKERS MAGAZINE what I have found from experience to be the requirements of a modern bank building, I feel I should start at the beginning, for such requirements are of more interest to those seeking a new home for an existing institution or those desirous of reconstructing an old building, which brings up the subject at once of location.

Primarily a bank should be a substantial structure and therefore, unless a special reason exists to the contrary, should occupy a prominent site, located on a main business thoroughfare, preferably a corner, immediately adjacent to its patrons and readily accessible by a cheap, quick means of transportation to outlying districts. Near the post office, if possible, is invariably very desirable for this purpose, as it becomes the centre of the town sooner or later.

The building externally should be distinctive, should look like a BANK and should call attention to itself by its substantial and conservative appearance. Its prominence is always largely enhanced by a contrast with its environments; that is, an individual building, if located among tall buildings or having a high office building above it, stands forth

Alterations to the First National Bank, Lexington, Virginia, 1914

Columbia Trust Company at Harlem, c1919

conspicuously. This subject is seldom given sufficient consideration, but if properly applied it is easily the best and cheapest bank advertising medium.

A bank building has a great advantage over an ordinary business building, in that its customers prefer, if practicable, to have an office under the same roof, reasoning that they will get better consideration by being known and will have many facilities afforded them in connection with the bank, and they are generally willing to pay larger rentals in consequence. This can often be seen where a bank office building is fully rented and adjoining business buildings are not so completely occupied.

The most important external requirement is that the building shall be devoid of anything appearing tawdry, vulgar or cheap. Every layman now knows that the old fashioned system of decorating the windows with large iron pipes to imitate impregnable protection is a pure fake and is no longer impressed by such a display, preferring a strong, substantial building to a flimsy jail. Well considered publicity is greater protection nowadays than small windows heavily laden with bogus bars that merely keep the inside concealed from the passer-by.

Only first-class material should be employed and if money is not plentiful, some other cheaper material should be adopted instead of an inferior quality of a more expensive substance, as such construction gives the impression of security. The best quality of granite, marble, limestone, brick, etc, can be used to create an eminently substantial looking building, if the whole be treated with skill. Anything of a perishable nature should under no circumstances be used, for such materials as zinc, tin, etc, soon present a dilapidated appearance, and thus indicate that poor taste has been employed in the construction of the building. This does not tend to inspire confidence in the bank's judgment in other matters that concern its customers.

A bank when going into a new building does so with the idea of making the new habitation its home for a long time and in consequence will suffer for any mistake made in its construction. For this reason untried innovations of materials, should be adopted only after very mature consideration.

Solidity cannot be too strongly impressed upon the outside of the building. As a principle this should always be employed. In such examples as the Bank of England and the National Bank of France this has been so well carried out that they are world famous for it.

An intending customer gets his first impressions of a bank's traditions and the character of its officers from its outward appearance and this should be made inviting to convey the desired impression of conservative enterprise, which alone will inspire confidence. For this reason, if a bank decides to rent its quarters, great care must be employed in the selection of the building under whose roof the institution makes its home, particularly so as the bank should be the soundest institution in its community. . . .

The material development of the country of late years has been so great that the demand for safe banking institutions has often run ahead of the local facilities, and in the effort to keep abreast of the times many obsolete systems and buildings have been allowed to exist long after they have ceased to be efficient. The building and the system are inseparable, and it is recognized that a new building should also stand for the discontinuance of out-of-date practices, and for the installation of all proved labor-saving arrangements, which signify money-making methods.

A modern bank should have all the latest electrical appliances which have proved superior to the old thick wall protection. A fully protected first-class building signifies the progressive spirit, which stands for the rapid handling of business at a reasonable cost, which has become so essential on account of the keen competition.

Like all branches of industry, a bank has to specialize more or less, and definite arrangements ought to be made to accomplish this. To meet these requirements, one who has made a special study of the entire banking question as applied to its home, and who would not allow one consideration to have undue prominence to the disadvantage of others,

Federal American National Bank, Washington, DC

can aid indefinitely in installing the bank in quarters that will be both economical and efficient in its conduct, signifying where savings may be made, or improvements incorporated at little expense.

With the banking situation as complicated as it is to-day, a banker can hardly keep pace with all the improvements introduced into the building, as well as in the operating of the bank itself, and by having competent advice the saving in time alone is considerable. The makers of various articles, and the experts on various details make the banker's life a burden if he attempts to decide all the points himself, unaided, or unadvised by an independent expert on the subject as a whole.

A substantial modern structure is an advertisement which it is difficult to overrate, and a desirable customer prefers to become associated with an institution located in a building of this character, one completely arranged with up-to-date vault equipment and protections, and all the improvements which modern practice has proved desirable and profitable.

From: 'The Requirements of a Modern Bank Building'. *Bankers Magazine*, Vol 83, No 11, Nov 1911, pp 658–662.

The Architect at Work

The 'Studio' publication of 1934, Building to the Skies, *remains Bossom's best known book. It was published in London after his return from his short but successful professional period in the USA. It summarised his architectural position outlining his own attitudes and theories, his philosophy and work methods. In his publication he placed his own work in the context of contemporary US developments. He wrote of his concern with 'time and progress' scheduling, site efficiency and building and erection techniques as well as issues that might more generously be described as those resting upon artistic principles.*

In a very real sense the book is a summary of the numerous articles he wrote for professional and commercial journals in the US and thus established at an earlier date a fairly complete record of his architectural career.

An architect in Canada or the United States, entrusted with the vast responsibility of designing a skyscraper, and seeing it through to its completion, has to be a good deal more than an architect of the traditional type.

He has to be a judge of land values and prospects. Before he can advise his client as to the height and capacity of the building best suited to the chosen location, he must make a social and economic study of the neighbourhood.

Is the district on the up-grade or otherwise? Can it support a twenty-storey building, or would one half that height be more appropriate? And the town itself? What are likely to be the movements of population within its boundaries? Is it growing away from or towards the selected site? How many houses and offices to let does it already contain? What are its industries, its transport facilities, the deposits in its banks, the outlook for its future trade and development? What, above all, does the American Telephone Company, that never anywhere looks less than seven years ahead, think of its prospects?

Alfred C. Bossom (left of centre with the moustache) with his staff in his Fifth Avenue office at the height of his American career.

All these are matters that have to be considered and resolved. Every busy and well-equipped architect's office on the other side of the Atlantic, assuming that he specialises in skyscrapers, has one or two members on his staff who are experts in just such problems and the answers to them, in city after city, and can safely report upon them. It is a side of his profession that qualifies him to act almost as a land agent or at least as a consultant on the wider business aspects of the relations between buildings and the community surrounding them.

I have more than once, while I was practising architecture in the United States, declined a commission to design a twenty-storey building for what I was convinced was only a six-storey town. In one case the owners of the site, a banking firm, disregarded my advice and engaged another architect to comply with their wishes. The building they desired was duly completed so far at any rate as the framework and the outer shell were concerned, and carried to the desired height. But not a single floor was ever put in above the sixth storey; the bank had completely overbuilt itself; its disastrously ill-judged expansion wrecked it.

No matter how good the design might have been, my reputation would have suffered through being connected with a building that was a commercial failure. That is why the designer of skyscrapers has always to think of the future of the projected building and to assess the chances of its bringing in a financial return to its owners before making up his mind whether to accept a commission. In that sense he must be something of a judge of business conditions, something of a financier, something of a specialist in the thousand and one factors that determine the rise or fall of any given locality, before he can sit down to his drawings and blue prints with the assurance that he has done the right thing.

I have been speaking, I notice, as though an architect's job began after a site had been procured by an owner anxious to embellish it with a skyscraper. But as a matter of fact it is a very common thing for a wealthy Canadian or American with a million dollars or so to invest, or for a firm that is outgrowing its quarters, to approach an architect with the request that he advise them as to the selection of a site and suggest what they should do with it.

In either case it is as an authority on the commercial possibilities and values of some plot of ground on a city street – a capacity in which the British architect is very rarely called upon to act – that the Transatlantic architect makes his first appearance on a scene that for the next eighteen months or so is to occupy his time and thoughts, day and night.

It was my custom after approving a site and the proposed methods of utilising it, and after giving the client a rough but substantially accurate estimate of what sort of structure would best satisfy his purposes and how much it would cost, to settle all the fundamental problems of the new building myself, to tabulate the results, turn them over to my designers, and then start a competition among them for their own ideas on the problem. I found this a capital method of encouraging keenness and the competitive spirit, and of bringing out whatever originality any member of the staff might have in him.

Even the smallest firms that undertook skyscraper work would employ from twenty to twenty-five draughtsmen. A larger firm would have perhaps sixty on its permanent staff and in busy times when a rush of commissions was on, this number might easily be doubled, with the men literally working day and night, and the architect himself, the hardest worker of them all, his suit case always packed, ready to start off on an inspection tour whenever his presence was required on some particular job, and resigned to spending at least ten nights in the month in a sleeping car. It was an intensely personal, responsible and absorbing life. With a regular salary list of, say, £3,000 a week, and permanent overheads amounting to some £50,000 a year, it could not have been anything else.

There are a hundred differences in the architectural practices of England and of America, both before and after a commission has been offered and

Alfred Bossom's New York studio.

accepted, and its terms agreed upon. One of them is that in the United States, and also in Canada, an architect treats his client much as a doctor treats his patient. Practically he prescribes the design that in his judgment will best meet the requirements of the case. He says in effect: "You ask us for a building most suitable to the location and to your needs. This is our idea of what it should be. It will cost you, as nearly as we can estimate, so much. It should be finished and ready for occupation in *x* number of months. Please let us know if you approve."

With these preliminaries settled and his design accepted, the architect gets busy on the drawings. For a relatively small, million-dollar building, two months ought to be enough for this. Bills of quantities are not used on the other side of the Atlantic and the drawings and specifications in consequence have to be extraordinarily precise and comprehensive. They show everything – every steel column, girder and plate, every pipe, every vent duct, every push button, every groove or chase for wiring or piping – everything. Separate sets, each complete in itself with detailed specifications attached, are made for the main sections of the job, such as excavation, steel work, lighting, heating, plumbing and ventilation. All told, they run into many hundreds.

From the moment he starts on his drawings, the skyscraper architect is in touch with structural engineers, contractors, manufacturers and suppliers of materials and with many of the heads of the thirty-two trades that will soon be working under him.

These informal but highly important exchanges are free of any obligation on either side. Those who are invited to attend them give their views and proffer their advice and suggestions freely and willingly – in the hope, of course, of getting a sub-contract but without any certainty, expressed or implied, that they will.

The architect is thus enabled to gather the latest information as to new processes, materials and inventions, market prices, the labour situation, the abundance or scarcity of supplies, and so on – all of which he utilises in his drawings, specifications, instructions, and so forth, as he goes along.

The corporate and co-operative spirit that runs through the Transatlantic building industries is very visible in all this. The architect is made entirely welcome to any item of special knowledge he is in search of and his prospective sub-contractors can supply. The feeling is that another skyscraper is a big event, and that it is to the general interest of everybody in the industry to help make it a success, even though their personal profit from the particular job on hand or their connection with it may ultimately prove to be nil.

Next to this practice of wide-range inquiry – a practice that is intensified as the work progresses – I should like to emphasise, as one more contrast with our British procedure, the fact that from start to finish full and detailed information is available at all times to everyone engaged on the job.

Frankness and a noonday publicity accompany every stage of the undertaking. The architect insists on being in complete possession of the owner's mind, intentions and desires. He in turn tells the owner everything. It is not until all the drawings and specifications are finished to the last screw-joint that contractors are invited to tender for the job or the general contract. They then know exactly what they are taking on and can pass on to the owner and the architect full details as to the sub-contractors they have in view.

As well as providing the competing general contractors with the full drawings and specifications, the architect, also, as a rule, sends them down to the local builders' exchanges so that sub-contractors in the vicinity of the projected building may study them and make their bid; and when the actual construction has begun the plans of the entire building are available in the contractor's shanty for anyone to see, and as the work proceeds a duplicate set is posted up on the appropriate floor, so that each operative may know what he is doing and why he is doing it and the exact nature of his contribution to the maelstrom of ordered activity that is storming all round him. . . .

If he is interested, and can read a blue-print, there is nothing to prevent a bricklayer's labourer, once on the job, from learning as much about it as the foreman himself. Timed to the minute months beforehand, all the operations that go to the erection of a skyscraper are as open and visible as the clock that records their progress.

Even the architect does not regard himself as an aloof and superior person. He is the generalissimo of the entire enterprise, but he visits the front, he is constantly in the trenches. Among the contractors, the superintendents and the builders' representatives, with whom he is regularly conferring, he is *primus inter pares*. He is their leader and

the ultimate court of appeal when a knotty problem has to be unravelled, but they are his colleagues. He or his representative is always on the job, always available, and never too conscious of omniscience to listen to suggestions.

It is on the competence and the personality of the architect and his ability to inspire respect and confidence not only among his immediate lieutenants, but among the polyglot hundreds who may be serving under him, that speedy, uninterrupted and efficient construction finally depends. Given the right quality of leadership, there is frequently developed throughout all ranks an enthusiasm to get the vast undertaking finished on time, a zeal and pride in their work, and a sense of adventurous toiling and good fellowship not exceeded, so far as I know, or at any rate not in civil life, in any other professional or industrial relationship. . . .

A skyscraper architect's life, as the huge undertaking moves to its conclusion, is one of exhausting anxiety and occasional friction. But he gets his reward now and then when he hears of mechanics stealing rides on trains to some town where he is known to be engaged on a new job and hiring a kit of standardised tools from the local pawnshop that they may be in a position to work under him again.

New Liberty Bank Building Typifies Spirit of New Buffalo

This article on the Liberty Bank Building erected in Buffalo, NY, in 1925 is typical of the promotional articles produced by Bossom himself for provincial newspapers. These contributions were all well measured, gently reminding the reader of the skill and competence of the architect involved and placing the comments in the context of a wider architectural framework.

Sited close by Sullivan's famous early terracotta faced skyscraper in downtown Buffalo, Bossom's own bank building, although less elegant and innovative and decorative than Sullivan's, still exerts a presence in the area with the twin silhouettes of the Statue of Liberty on its pointed roofs. Today the building is as much a landmark in the centre of Buffalo as both its predecessors and successors. The Buffalo Sunday Times *article included here in full expressed well the architect's own sentiment in visualising power and enterprise.*

Visualizing power and enterprise, there looms on the skyline of Buffalo the tallest structure in the northern part of the Empire State – the Liberty Bank. From its foot-hold on the living rock to the stately figures on its towers, it typifies the spirit of a community.

Close to Buffalo's splendid proposed civic center, and near beautiful McKinley Monument and Lafayette Square, the Liberty Bank naturally required monumental treatment. Its site measures 232 feet in Court Street and 61 feet in Pearl and Main. This huge rectangular area is one of the most important pieces of real estate in the city. Naturally the bankers desired to make the most of it; to utilize it not only for their own advantage, but for serving the best interests of Buffalo.

Banking has become more and more complex as it meets the needs of twentieth century business. It must aid other enterprises to develop their resources. As an eminent financier, the late A B Hepburn, so wisely observed, 'The bank makes money by helping others to make money.' Over every financial institution might well be written that motto from a princely crest, 'I Serve'.

Expresses Bank's Ideals

The Liberty Bank desired to have a structure expressive of its ideals of public service. The dominant motif of this lofty pile is that of the Liberty Bank as a factor in the busy life of the municipality. A sense of freedom and democracy is expressed in the design. As Buffalo is known the world over for her deep appreciation of the fine arts, the Liberty Bank, occupying so prominent a location, would be expected to be responsive to the public taste.

The writer considers it, therefore, an honor to have this opportunity to describe what might be called the development of the design of Buffalo's tallest building.

The necessity of utilizing to the full the valuable plot of real estate, such as that on which the Liberty Bank is built, required that we should have not merely three or four stories, but 23. Out of such a need has developed American vertical architecture as distinguished from the horizontal seen in European cities where the streets are narrower and great height is not practicable.

Mr G Topham Forrest, supervising architect of the London County Council, who recently made a survey of the urban architecture of the United States, recites that all American cities, such as New York and Buffalo, are some 700 miles nearer the equator than is London. Therefore, the angle of the sun's rays at most periods of the day is such that they penetrate into all parts of the building and are not obstructed by surrounding buildings. This reason, if there were no economic equation, justifies the vertical in all our architectural design. As the Liberty Bank is so unusually favourably situated, there are comparatively few structures near it which approach its height. It is 332 feet tall, counting from the curb to the summit of the tower. The composition of the design is held together by two towers. The observer who views it from either end gets a vision of tapering grace, while the broader side shows dignity and solidity.

Of Liberty Bank Period

Architects who are asked to describe a building are frequently asked, 'To what period does it belong?' The answer to this might be that this structure is of the Liberty Bank Period. Essentially on account of its monumental character and of the wish to suggest a sense of security and power as well as beauty of form, the outlines are classic.

Coming into the city of Buffalo on a steamer, the writer was deeply impressed by the similarity between this entrepot of the Great Lakes and the ancient city of Alexandria. There is indeed a remarkable parallel between Buffalo and the wonder city of old. Alexandria, it will be remembered, was the port to which the grain from granaries of Egypt were brought for shipment, and as is the case with Buffalo, traded with all the world. Both cities have splendid natural harbours which have been developed with highest engineering skill. Alexandria had, as Buffalo has, an enormous breakwater to give refuge for vessels. On an island in her harbour it will be remembered that there once stood a tall structure known as the Pharos, lighthouse, treasury, and citadel. On the summit burned a beacon said to have been visible 70 miles at sea. Your modern Alexandria of the Lakes, thought the writer, might well have to its tallest building a suggestion of classic glory. One of the Seven Wonders of the World, the Pharos rests like a wraith of the past upon your Liberty Bank.

It has been said by critics and students that the Liberty Bank building shows an influence of the Adam Brothers, which means after all its design was conceived in the classic spirit – of simplicity and dignity.

Design is Original

The design of the Liberty Bank building is original in that it is adapted to a special site, to the requirements of an American institution, and to the ideals of the city of Buffalo itself.

While on a brief visit to the Exposition Internationale des Arts Decoratifs et Industriels Modernes, the writer found many reflexes of what

might be termed the American or un-American vertical architecture. Some of the pavilions in this mighty display on the Seine, which has been organized through the unselfish public spirit of the Republic of France, were designed with long, sure lines with definite termination, and in fact, with the same general idea as that which we have endeavored to put into the design of the Liberty Bank. The great lesson of the Paris Exposition is that it accentuates beauty of form and of outline and minimizes mere ornament. This is exactly what has been sought in the designing of the Liberty Bank. It was designed as a whole; detail has been subordinated to the general effect.

From: *The Buffalo Sunday Times*, Aug 23, 1925, p 64.

America's National Architecture

Alfred Bossom expressed a great interest in the idea of a specific American architecture, an architecture, that is, that expressed indigenous cultural connections and national aspirations. He drew the analogy that European architectures were generally based on national requirements which produced horizontal axes, 'whereas America's main compositions have the vertical as the principal axis and so it has been largely a matter of detail only wherein America has borrowed from the European precedents . . .' Such arguments as these were vigorously used by Bossom to justify the skyscraper buildings for the burgeoning new business districts in the expanding towns of the United States during the first part of this century. His articles on national architecture were written at the end of the first quarter century, and thus fit contextually into this wider concern shared by many other practising architects and theorists at the time. Through such ideas and articles American business architecture came to maturity. The following two articles both published in the American Architect *convey Bossom's ideas at the time.*

A national architecture is not one copied from some other country on account of its beauty alone. In the extreme, the Laplander has built his igloo or the native of Hindu China his rice-straw tent to meet climatic conditions. So have other famous architectures been built up. But they have followed a precedent, and this has been used as the basis of upbuilding of every great distinctively national architecture.

Ictinus, Bramante, Michaelangelo, and Sir Christopher Wren all took advantage of what had gone before. Architecture is distinctive in this sense from the other arts, for, not only is it a matter of beauty but it also has to conform to many physical requirements to be successful. The painter can turn a picture upside down and it affects no one but himself, but the architect creating a house without stairs or roof will have perpetrated the useless. Precedent on both the practical and aesthetic sides is inseparable from a successful national architecture.

For years the claim has been that America should have her own national architecture, – one indigenous to herself, and by force of circumstances America has developed a type of building which was never built outside of her borders. But, as regards precedent. What does this mean? It means that other minds who have had similar problems to study, have developed certain results and in continuation, we build upon their thought foundations. Refinements are introduced. Theories are carried a step further, but all along the path of progress.

Rome in the heyday of her conquering success did not have the remarkable opportunity that the United States has today, but she did create a national style. Why has America not done so? Due to the demand for tremendous quantity and appalling speed, American architects have largely turned to the countries whose work has been the more illustrated or studied. Trade routes and pleasure pilgrimages have covered Europe with American visitors. There is hardly an unknown building in the Old World. In fact, it is to be doubted if there are not better records of the architecture of certain European states in America than they have at home. Thus almost out of necessity, the heavily pressed architects of America have by instinct delved among the precedents of Europe in the solution of their problems and the world's verdict is that they have achieved remarkable success therefrom.

European architectures generally were all based upon their national requirements and had their principal axes horizontal, whereas America's main compositions have the vertical as the principal axes and so it has been largely a matter of detail only wherein America has borrowed from the European precedents. Climatic influences throughout Europe were not similar to those here. In Europe the object was to keep out the weather, the cold and rain. In America, our desire is to let the weather in, – to keep us cool. Italian work had its great wall surfaces – beautiful indeed, but commercially America is compelled to have the reverse, with great window spaces, the wall being suppressed.

The Greeks had a stateliness incompatible with the American temperament. In fact all had to meet their own conditions. A national architecture should be a portrait in stone and brick of a type of life and the form of activity lived by the people, and in the hands of America's very clever designers, marvellous buildings have been conceived and constructed based on the European motives. But hasn't America got an artistic heritage of her own? Hasn't she a cultural background as complete as any country in the world? Didn't the men on this continent pour out their souls' efforts in the creation of vast buildings at the same time the men in Europe were doing it?

In the early centuries of the Christian era, the Mayans in Yucatan, a people who probably migrated to this continent from Asia five or six thousand years ago with little or no traceable artistic instincts and who by the influences of nature, atmospheric, geographic, etc, evolved an architectural art of their own as complete as that of any European country. This American native architecture grew to great perfection, but due to difficult climatic conditions, the unpopularity of travelling in countries with revolutionary habits, Mexico and Central America have not been investigated or studied to any great degree. The archaeologist is almost alone in his work. The artistic side has been more or less incidentally investigated until quite recently.

An architect starting a new design is practically compelled to refer to the creations of his predecessors and no client would thank an architect who ignored the consideration of the experience that others had gained. Precedent due to good printing is more available than ever, and rightly so for it enables the architect to have a better idea of how his complete design will appear. He is not experimenting so much and great investments are not imperiled by uncertainties, at least, not beyond a certain point. . .

Within her borders America covers a range of climatic requirements from the sub-Artic to the sub-tropic and almost every form of life is lived within them, in consequence, but without exception the climate is clear, the sky is bright, and the air is stimulating and people are excessively active. There is a consistency in the type of life lived in America more complete than found in any other area on the earth's surface among a hundred million people.

America has been called "the melting pot," though in reality it is nature showing superiority over man which has thereby caused a similar type of life to be lived by all citizens. Class distinctions are quite unimportant and transportation is freer than anywhere on the surface of the globe. Hence, if a natural style were to take form it would grow with far greater speed and would come to a state nearing perfection more quickly due to the tremendous number of minds thinking along parallel lines at the one time and seeing the results of their fellows.

The Mayan work is shrouded in mystery. It is safe to assume that by the second century AD they had developed a definite culture which grew until between the sixth and the eighth centuries. The people at that time probably suffered from some terrible pestilence but came back in about the eleventh century and continued until about the fourteenth when some other catastrophe apparently overcame them. Due to the seasons in Guatemala and Yucatan, a white man has not been able to stay long comfortably in these places, and to reach them to study the arts there. He has had to fight a great natural barrier of ungoverned vegetation, through trackless places and to face malaria. This naturally has prevented intensive study of the great works that were created and so the records of these are still comparatively meagre...

They were essentially original, as are the American people by nature today. Their sense of composition resulted from a natural evolution. As the Greeks had their style of architecture, so the Mayans had theirs. Not based upon a fixed proportion, but based upon certain principles which can be modified to meet any requirements such as are indispensable today in the development of America's twentieth century architecture.

These motifs could be carried on from where they were left. The Tikel pyramid in Guatemala studied by Maudsley is an example of a typical vertical composition. Chichen-Itza, Copan, Palenque, all had buildings of a similar nature. They, like their successors, used the vertical as the principal axes of their compositions for they always set their palaces and their priestly temples on the summits of great stylobates which stood hundreds of feet in the air. They set these back terrace upon terrace for the obvious structural reason and their natural desire to obtain a beautiful outline. We know they used color, as many examples have come down to us. They realized that the silhouette of their building read itself against the sky. Hence, they gave, perhaps, more consideration to detail than any other people.

They crowned their structure with pierced combs made of stone knowing that a tall structure had no back and could be seen from everywhere. For, when a building stands one hundred or more feet in the air its outline cannot be hidden.

We, in America, have realized that it is not selfishness, but stupidity to carry up a tall building perfectly square to its maximum height. It was natural that this should have been done in the early days, but it has been slowly realized that for self preservation equity with the other people is advantageous. Light and air, the essentials of human life, compelled the setting back form of architecture.

It is interesting to compare some of the early canyons of New York with those of Yucatan, and those of the Southlands are much nearer what the zoning law is going to compel here in the North. In fact the building law today is making us do what these people did of their own volition, of course, in modified form and to meet different requirements. But it is a very small step from the Tikal pyramid at Guatemala to a zoning law building of Broadway.

From: 'America's National Architecture', *American Architect*, Vol 128, Jul 29, 1925, pp 77–83 (Reprinted in *The Architect*, Aug 21, 1925).

Fifty Years' Progress Toward an American Style in Architecture

Had there been no Plymouth Rock, nor Jamestown, nor St Augustine, nor Santa Barbara, there would have been no question as to whether or not an American style of architecture was our goal.

Architecture is of the soil, the air and the customs of a country. It springs from the needs of a race. It is a portrait in stone of the type of life lived. If a people be at business all day; dines at public restaurants, and wanders in the dancing pavilions of Jazzmania all night, it needs an entirely different architectural setting from that needed by feudal lords who fought enemies and guarded themselves night and day against attack and surprise. As architecture more and more meets the requirements of life; as the rearing of its cottages or castles or skyscrapers is controlled by the culture a nation develops, if true, it automatically becomes a style. If the American people were not of the melting pot, if it had emerged from protoplasm to Pelmanism all of itself, it would now have architecture which would have been as much of it as a shell is of the oyster it shelters.

Suppose, there existed in this continent a race, which at first lived in caves to protect itself from bears and panthers; then grew stronger and dared to live more in the open, to depend upon its weapons to resist attack, and finally took to building forts and houses, and eventually palaces? What have they left? There were on this continent, in fact long before Columbus, peoples who were much the same horizon of culture as the archaic Greeks. If Mound Builders, Mayas, Toltecs, Aztecs, the subjects of the Incas, had not been put out of their stride by certain Europeans who "discovered" them, they would have probably gone onward and upwards and developed more of art, literature, science and all the finer embellishments of civilization than any other people. Then there would have been an American style in construction independent of all orders, and developed without light from any lamps of architecture kindled in other climes.

Of course, no type of national architecture can throw aside all that has been developed since the world began; every country is susceptible to foreign architectural influences. There can, for all that, be no question but what the United States is more than merely groping its way toward an architecture of its own. It is progressing though with travail of spirit, because it is trammeled in so many ways by the traditions of the lands from which its many racial strains originally sprang . . .

How the American skyscraper has grown in height and in the favor of man since the days when the first was reared on the shores of Lake Michigan! When I arrived in New York in 1903 the building for the New York *World*, with its gilded dome, topped the urban landscape. Today it is almost buried among the lower stratum of buildings. The present structures in its vicinity have reached such a height that the skyscraper of even twenty years ago looks like a cottage in an Alpine valley.

But, after all, it is not the altitude nor yet the extent of the tall building which makes it so worthy of its place in the American architecture of the future. True American architecture must build from the inside out, from center to perimeter. It concerns itself with use before the overcoat shown to the passerby.

An American skyscraper is like a human being in its organization. Just as the Greeks in making their columns are credited with copying the proportions of the human form divine, so the tall building of the United States is the whole body. It has its skeleton of steel; its arteries through which course heat; its soil pipes for the elimination of its wastes; its veins which supply its water; its tingling electric nerves of sensation and communication, such as its cables for its telephones; its circulatory system; its ventilating plant or lungs for air; its batteries of elevators which make possible the stream of pulsing life. It has in its outer walls of masonry the muscles and last of all, its clothes on which are its details of decoration and adornment.

Every outline of the tall buildings of the states, centers of co-operative activity, is usually controlled absolutely by the purposes for which it is intended. Now that in some two hundred and sixty-one American cities there are zoning laws which regulate the height of the skyscraper, it is acquiring even greater beauties of line and form. The distinguished architect of the London County Council, G Topham Forrest, whose report on the architecture of urban America has recently been published, says that the terraced or "set-back" formation which now limits altitude, has resulted in a signal improvement in the form of American big buildings. He was kind, for some of those created after the first rush have fittingly been called packing cases with windows. The ingenuity and imagination required to adapt the skyscraper to the new regulations have made for new beauties and for yet more novel nuances of charm. The tall American building, therefore, quite aside from its garments and draperies of stone or terra cotta, or what you will, has a distinctive artistic merit due to its very adaptability to the purpose intended, which obviously is the greatest step toward a distinctive style so far made in the United States of America.

There is scarcely any detail, for instance, on that splendid fabric, the Shelton Hotel, and there is an indwelling and ineffable grace about it which is due to its being planned as a mass, rather than in obedience to the mincing and meticulous demands of a period. It may be said, perhaps, to have something of a North Italian influence, but in every respect I shall call it American of the truest type. Of such structures as these it may well be said that they were conceived in truth and then designed in beauty.

What, then, shall be the treatment of our American architecture, so bold and so original in meeting the requirement of a complex civilization? The Woolworth Building, the creation of Cass Gilbert, has a Gothic panoply, and it is a Cathedral of Commerce in name and guise. It is thoroughly American in its utilization of space, its convenience, in its engineering, and certainly it is one of the many monuments to American achievement. It is well ornamented, even lavishly, but still it is American.

The Municipal Building, looking across City Hall Park at the Woolworth, is a combination of Renaissance from Italy and Sir Christopher Wren. An American composition indeed, and possessing great beauty, its detail is all drawn from European motifs.

The Bush Building is another phase of Gothic adapted to American composition and the Magnolia Building of Dallas is purely American, though its details first saw the light on the shores of the Mediterranean. Many other buildings of American form could be cited but the point in mind is that the steps toward an American style have been along the lines of composition and not through the medium of the trimmings and detail generally.

Before the passage of the regulations restricting height, some most heinous offenses against good taste and the laws of proportion were committed in the name of this nascent American architecture. It was believed that in some way or other the fronts of these new types of buildings should be ornamented. Why this belief nobody professes really to know, but the Grand Architect of the Universe might attribute it to human inertia. The skyscrapers no longer needed marble columns or the support of them. The wonderful maze of pillars in a Gothic cathedral were needed in order to keep the heavy roof from spreading the walls, and the flying buttresses guarded against similar disaster. Even the classic pilasters were not merely ornaments in the old orders of architecture, but they were braces as well. In both these beautiful Old World styles of architecture decoration grew out of the employment of stone as a necessary support. When that need had disappeared and masonry became a mere shell, the architects found it hard to adapt themselves to the new conditions. Just as for many years coaches on the steam railroads had whip sockets, although the iron horse needed no lash – so the ornamentations of the horizontal architecture of Europe are still being applied to our American architecture.

Thus perched high on some cloud-piercing office building, we even now see Grecian temples; and so far above our heads that they can scarcely be made out with the naked eye, appear florid scrolled decorations of the Italian Renaissance. Garlands and pot bellied cupids and sad marble ladies holding up cornices are thrust upon walls where they serve no purpose and can scarcely be seen.

It is desirable, however, that the skyscraper of today should have some attractive outer garments and since this is so, why not have them native American? It is not generally recognized – more is the pity – that there existed in this hemisphere an important architecture long before the coming of Columbus. Along the western coasts were aborigines of a more advanced culture who had vast apartment houses or cliff dwellings. The earliest natives of Mexico lived in houses of tuffa or adobe or stone – which had pointed arched doors and not too many windows – the architecture of which in many ways resembled Gothic. In Mexico City were ornate temples and altars and further south in Central America and along the western base of the Andes were impressive examples of building. The glory of this American architecture, however, was the Mayan, important examples of which were found by the Spanish Conquistadores and are being daily revealed to us through exploration and research.

Whatever may have been the origin of the Mayas, they of all peoples on the American continents had reached the highest civilization and made the most progress in the arts and sciences. Originating their culture in Central America, they had migrated from Guatemala toward the north, and generally spread into Yucatan, where they were overwhelmed in the course of a great development of their civilization either by plague or warlike enemies.

What better evidence of the architectural skill of the Mayans can be found than the pyramids and temples and monuments they left behind them? They were the just masters of vertical architecture, for they loved to meet and worship on great heights of their own creation. Compare these Mayan pyramids as photographed by Maudslay, the English explorer, and in models at the Smithsonian Institution, with the present day, set-back American skyscraper. The resemblance is a startling one. These pyramids were terraced three or four times or more, and their summits were reached by a long flight of steps. The American skyscraper of today has elevators and its shell construction permits it to have plenty of room inside. All their ornamentation was in such proportion, that they might well be used as motifs for the larger structures now being erected in our large American cities. In fact, a comparison of a restoration of the Tikal pyramid built by Mayan hands in Guatemala with a combination loft and office building thirty stories in height shows that America is doing by law what originally man in Mexico did by desire.

America is at the cross roads in her architectural development. She has not progressed as regards her domestic work, and the great contribution for better or worse and upon which the American architects for the last fifty years must stand is the tall building. In that new mass composition have been created works original, daring and, I feel, partly accredited as being a successful contribution to the world's artistic growth – but the speed with which these are needed due to the great interest charges and anxiety on the part of owners to start the flow of income into their own pockets,

Two recent photographs (see also p 90) of the Petroleum Building, Houston, Texas. (Photo: Paul Hester)

have compelled the architects to use reference books *ad nauseam*. If this is to continue with respect, the chance of a great art arising is slim, but if the natural pride in individuality of the American owner can be aroused, the American architect has demonstrated his desire to use the best there is in him, leaving to posterity a group of buildings which will justly do credit to the great period through which we are passing.

From 'Fifty Years' Progress Toward an American Style in Architecture', *American Architect*, Vol 129, No 2488, Jan 5, 1926, pp 43–49.

The Romance of the Skyscraper

Amongst Bossom's papers was found the following short synopsis of an address he gave to the 'Friends of America' in December 1943 at Portsmouth which nicely rounds off his retrospective view of his work as an architect, in relation to his historic interests and influences and his underlying love for the technical efficiency of good building. This paper has never been previously published.

'We shape our buildings and afterwards our buildings shape us' said the Prime Minister in speaking of the restoration of the British House of Commons, and nowhere is this more significant than in America where the growth of its people and buildings has been both strong and vigorous.

From the wigwam, stockaded fortress and log cabin to the graceful and charming developments of Colonial architecture and then, during the last fifty years, into the Age of Invention which brought in its train that great contribution to constructive development, the skyscraper, American architecture has expressed the growth of a young and energetic nation which has freed itself from the trammels of the past, grown rich in self-expression and allowed its spirit to soar to unanticipated heights.

In all ages and in all countries the greatest architecture has, of course, been inspired, and very often religious worship has been its basis. This was the case with the Parthenon at Greece, the Pantheon in Italy, the Temple of Karnac in Egypt, Santa Sophia in Turkey and our Salisbury Cathedral. The American skyscraper in its way, too, was inspired, for Americans worship success and these were their shrines of prosperity.

Any thriving organisation, be it a firm, bank or family, built its own skyscraper. It proclaimed to the world the success of its owner. There is the great Rockefeller Centre, the Astor and Vanderbilt Hotels and the Carnegie, Chrysler and Woolworth Buildings – in fact, one can go right down the line and there they stand, colossal pylons proclaiming the prosperity of these people!

The skyscraper has given the United States the opportunity of making one of the greatest contributions to world progress. Though, most emphatically, skyscrapers are not wanted in England on account of our climate and geographical position, nevertheless, the development of these great structures, costing such fabulous amounts of money, in a country where men appreciate the financial value of time, have entirely revised the science of building.

The world owes to these buildings the principles of factory-assembly (I won't use the word prefabrication), and by this system anything up to between 70 per cent to 80 per cent of the materials going into these buildings can be completed in comfortably heated and ventilated factories, and then taken to the site for assembly. Factory-assembly means that many of the units making up a building are assembled in sections in factories and brought complete to the site and there joined and fitted together like a Meccano set, and, by following a

Time and Progress Schedule, no time is wasted in waiting.

America has done away with the law of Ancient Lights. Skyscrapers have no party walls, so that literally the day the land is purchased and a company or individual decides to erect a building, work can be started immediately. Skyscrapers are of such economic and scientific development that 42 out of 48 States in America have insisted on some form of registration of architects to ensure that the men designing skyscrapers shall be fully qualified and capable of doing the work. The sciences of steel erection, plumbing, heating, artificial lighting and ventilation, all owe their greatest developments to these architectural mammoths which have, with their fine materials and good workmanship, stimulated the finest progress in the building industry.

The skyscraper was largely made possible by applying the unusual principle of using a structural material in tension. The first design for one of these buildings was made by a Milwaukian named Buffinger who, in 1887, was granted a patent for his plan though, in the end, no skyscraper was ever built from his designs. Nevertheless, the ideas were seized upon and have since developed far beyond his first dreams. This novel form of construction was made possible by:

(1) The development of the rolled steel beam, of which Andrew Carnegie was the great producer, and which was used to form the skeleton of the skyscraper;
(2) Roebling's invention of the wire rope which made a high-speed lift or elevator possible; and
(3) Francis H Kimball's adaption of the caisson principle for the foundation work of buildings.

Added to these were Thomas Eddison's innumerable electrical developments which gave good light; Bell's introduction of the telephone to help communication, and all the other up-to-date paraphenalia providing good heating, ventilation and sanitary arrangements.

Many state that skyscrapers were possible on account of the rock foundations underlying New York, but this is not so for they started in Chicago and were largely the result of rapidly acquired wealth. The Americans react quickly to new impressions; they are willing to experiment with anything new and instinctively love competition, and, the skyscraper performed the dual role of not only announcing great success and prosperity to the world at large, but also of itself earning substantial dividends. The first of the mammoth skyscrapers was the Singer Sewing Machine Building, 612ft high and 92ft below ground, which was such an advertisement to the world at large that during the first year, additional profits flowing in from China alone are credited to have paid for the building.

The work of the pioneers in this different method of building has brought quicker and cheaper results without requiring operatives to work harder or longer and, at the same time, permitting them to earn higher wages on account of better organisation, and, at the same time, yielding greater dividends to the owners concerned. This has been brought about by:

(1) The thorough organisation of each enterprise from its inception to its completion;
(2) The preparation of complete drawings and of all details before work was undertaken;
(3) Obtaining full competition upon all subcontracts forming part of the structure; and
(4) The rigid application of the Time and Progress Schedule.

We have a lot to learn from the American general system of organisation for, in addition to real leadership on the part of those in charge of the construction work, there were no secrets about the job. Everyone was informed as to what was to come next, and the system of supervision was complete, from the time the Schedule stated the first spadeful of earth was to be turned, to the start and finish of every other job going to make the finished building. Looking back, I remember the first 20-storey building, 250ft high, the First National Bank of Richmond, Virginia, which in 1909, took exactly nine months to build. It took three months to put in the foundations on the bank of the James River, and six months later it was finished exactly as required by the Time and Progress Schedule.

Many people think that as these skyscrapers are so large, their cubic cost is more than that of our buildings in England. As a matter of fact, our great commercial undertakings cost exactly the same as theirs per foot cube, though, in America during pre-war days, the bricklayers were paid five times as much as were the bricklayers here. Carpenters, plumbers, stonemasons, were paid three-and-a-half times as much, yet, the total cost was the same. This was accomplished by the methods aforementioned.

The laws controlling these buildings were constantly kept up-to-date and were very simple, and the buildings were so financed that after about 30 years they had paid for themselves. This was the result of teamwork: the owner, architect, builder, mechanics, all working together to make the job a success.

In the early days owners tried to overcrowd their sites by putting too large a building on the land. This led to the era known as the 'Canyons of Broadway', when, to walk down lower New York did seem like wandering in great gaps between tremendously high cliffs! To alter this principle, architects got together and evolved what amounted to a 'zoning law', stating which sort of building and to what use it should be put, could be erected in different parts of a town. It was also arranged that every building should fit inside certain planes, or an 'envelope' as it were, so that everyone would know exactly how big a building could be legally, and so on. Similar rulings should apply in this country.

This modernising of our laws and methods, and the giving to our people a proper technical education and every mechanical device to help make their work easier will greatly reduce the cost of our pre-war buildings. It will help us to build more quickly; it will give our workers better wages, and, of course, if we can do this in the building industry, it can also be done in other industries throughout the country, and thus enable our men to get back to work when they return from the Forces and factories.

From: An Address by Bossom to the 'Friends of America' on 'The Romance of the Skyscraper' in the Portsmouth Training College on Friday 17 Dec 1943.

The Editor

Dennis Sharp is an architect in private practice in London; critic, author and lecturer. He trained as an architect at the Architectural Association School, London and at Liverpool University, where he was Leverhulme Fellow in Architecture from 1960–63. He was Architect and Technical Officer, Civic Trust for the North West for a year, prior to his appointment as Lecturer in Architecture, Manchester University, in 1964.

In 1968 he became General Editor and Senior Lecturer at the AA London, where he remained until 1982 and now serves as a Council Member. In 1981 he was a Visiting Professor at Columbia University, New York. He has lectured extensively across the USA as well as in Europe and Asia. He was appointed a Distinguished Visiting Scholar by the University of Adelaide, South Australia, 1984.

Dennis Sharp is also a Director of the International Committee of Architectural Critics (CICA) and author of a number of books on modern architecture, including, *A Visual History of Twentieth Century Architecture*, which appears in a newly revised edition in 1984.

Mr Sharp's interest in Lord Bossom began when he compiled a special issue of the *AA Quarterly* magazine on 'Anglo-American Connections' with research assistant *Peter Wylde* who is jointly responsible for the research on this volume.